Practical Primary Science

Practical Primary Science

Romola Showell

WLE
Ward Lock Educational

First published 1983
by Ward Lock Educational Ltd
47 Marylebone Lane
London W1M 6AX

A Ling Kee Company

ISBN 0 7062 4240 8

British Library Cataloguing in Publication Data

Showell, Romola
Practical primary science
1. Science—Study and teaching (Elementary)
I. Title
372.3'5 LB1585

ISBN 0–7062–4240–8

Typeset in Great Britain by Inforum Ltd, Portsmouth.
Printed in Finland by K J Gummerus Osakeyhtö.

Contents

Preface

There are still many primary teachers who, because of their own limited knowledge, feel nervous about introducing science into the curriculum of their schools. Those who did not enjoy school science lessons often have rather hazy recollections of complicated chemistry and physics experiments and think that their own inadequacies will prevent them from successfully developing science in the classroom. However, science is a subject in which the enthusiastic teacher can learn with the children and, in any case, almost all teachers are actually doing science already without necessarily realizing it.

In the primary school, science should be a highly practical subject in which children learn to observe accurately, to devise experiments in order to find the answers to problems, and to record in a scientific manner, however simply, what they have found out. As they mature, they will begin also to develop the ability to communicate their findings to others and to make reasoned deductions from the results of their investigations. Science, even in its elementary stages, is an exact subject but its scope for the primary child is vast and, if presented properly, these early lessons will form the basis of the more advanced studies that the pupil will encounter later. It is in the primary classroom that the beginnings of a permanent interest may take root.

This book is intended for any primary teacher who wants some ideas for starting science. It is not intended to be an overall syllabus nor does it try to cover all the possible areas available, but it presents a series of topics which could be used, with adaptation, for primary children of any age. It is hoped that, after trying out some of these topics, the teacher will be able to appreciate the elements of science in many of the activities already carried out in the school and will be able to make the best of opportunities as they arise.

Some primary schools already have a very definite science syllabus; many of the suggested topics will fit in with this and may suggest some new ideas for presentation. For those teachers who feel that all subjects should be integrated, rather than kept in rigid compartments, links with other subjects have been indicated so that science can be seen as one part of the whole curriculum.

Introduction

GENERAL NOTES

1 Although the ideas in this book are presented as a series of separate topics, it is intended that they should be seen as starters for more concentrated work developed over a reasonable period of time.
2 Traditionally science in schools has been divided into biology, chemistry and physics. For primary children, however, these divisions are too structured. Although the topics contain elements of these subjects, they also include mathematics, geology and environmental studies; the obvious links with such subjects as geography, history and craft can be seen in many of them.
3 All science should be practical and should be introduced in such a way that the children can see why they are doing experiments and making observations. No two teachers will work in the same way; it is up to each one to decide whether the work should be done by the whole class or as a group activity. However it is organized, it can reasonably be divided into

a. Introduction — a talk, a demonstration, a visit, a particular event, a specific sample or specimen.
b. Discussion with the children about the topic so that a decision can be made as to how the work will be carried out.
c. Organization of necessary resources or activities and detailed planning of the topic — time-scale, class or group activities, the work of each group, final outcome.
d. Doing the work.
e. Recording the observations.
f. Putting the work together and exhibiting or displaying so that the children can see it as a whole.
g. Evaluation.

4 The recording of the work is essential if science, as a primary subject, is to be treated seriously. The method will vary according to age, ability and the requirements of the teacher, but it should be done in some way.

a. Talking — the child talking to the teacher, to a group or to the class; using tape recordings.
b. Writing — from a single word caption to a structured piece of descriptive prose.

c. Graphic and three-dimensional presentation — painting, drawing, modelling, tabulating, charting.
d. Photography.
e. Demonstration (e.g., how to make a windmill or a model water-wheel).
f. Annotated collection of specimens or a series of experiments.

5 If a child has taken the trouble to do his or her best work, some trouble should be taken to see that it is recognized in some way by showing it to the rest of the class, to the school or to visitors to the school. It is also worth considering keeping individual and group topic books as part of the class library. Many of these make good, simple reference books and are often overlooked once the particular project is finished.

ORGANIZATION

While some primary schools have specialized rooms for science and other practical subjects, others have to make use of the everyday classroom and so have to cope with the problems of storage and lack of work space. It must be stressed that science can be taught anywhere and resources can be kept within reasonable limits. In this book, I have kept suggestions for expensive apparatus to a minimum. This is purely for economic reasons and not because there is any particular merit in using home-made materials; it is perfectly possible to use and adapt cheap or throw-away items and so keep the money that is available for the purchase of good reference books and the pieces of apparatus for which there is no adequate substitute (e.g., microscopes, mirrors, accurate timers and balances).

The use of workcards and worksheets is the choice of the individual teacher but, if the work is well planned and the children know exactly what is expected of them, they should not be necessary. However, if they are used they should be made for the particular group in mind, they should be well presented, they should not be too limiting and, above all, they should not be used as a substitute for practical work.

APPARATUS AND EQUIPMENT

1 Much of the apparatus needed is to be found in any primary school; such things as plastic pots and bottles, cooking foil and tins can be collected quite easily. There are, however, some items of apparatus that will have to be purchased, although many of them can also be used for other subjects. These include

Tools — hammers, pliers, small hacksaws, screwdrivers, hand forks, trowels
Aquaria — several small plastic ones are better than one large glass one
Good glass hand lenses
Sets of plastic measures
Seconds timers
Flower pots and seed trays
Scales and balances
Plastic bowls and trays
Thermometers — room, clinical, soil
Mirrors
Electric kettle — for the teacher's use only, but it is useful to have a means of heating water for some experiments.

2 Some desirable, but not essential, items include

Binocular microscopes
Seed propagator
Animal cages.

3 Young children cope very well with audiovisual equipment and nowadays some primary schools have access to microcomputers as well as the more commonly used items. Part of their science work should include training in the use of such things as tape recorders and slide, film-strip and overhead projectors so that they can use these for recording their work or communicating their findings to other children.

4 Reference books — as many as possible — will be needed. These ought to be both accurate and readable; even books with texts that are beyond the ability of a particular group may well have valuable illustrations or can be used with the help of the teacher.

RESOURCES

Making use of all the available resources makes the teaching of science much easier, but it is all too easy to overlook some of the following, less obvious possibilities.

1 Books and other written materials — magazines, comics, newspapers, pamphlets, brochures, advertisements, mail-order catalogues. The ability to use a library and to appreciate the importance of reference books is needed for any subject and is not exclusive to science.

2 Objects — any items that can be used to exploit scientific ideas — bicycle, flying toys, collections of rocks or metals, simple machines.

3 People — experts with specialized knowledge, craftsmen, people with a particular skill or interest.
4 Audiovisual facilities — slides, film strips, films, video tapes, television and radio programmes.
5 Places — museums, zoos, safari parks, nature trails, natural sites (i.e. parks, fields, woodland, hedgerows, streams, seashore), historical sites, buildings, workshops.
6 Sources of information — there are many of these and a list of useful addresses can be found in Section 21.

USING THE BOOK

Each topic is presented in the same way.

1 An introductory paragraph outlining the content.
2 General notes of background information for the teacher.
3 Activities and experiments for the children.
4 Ways in which the topic could be developed further.
5 Possible links with other subject areas.
6 Resources — information books, special apparatus, visits, visual aids, sources of information.

Primary children are enthusiastic; work that interests and stimulates them will bring out the best results. Whatever work they do should be worthwhile with a definite aim in mind, and whatever information they are given should be accurate. If you do not know the answers, admit it and make use of good reference books, or devise work so that you and the children do the finding out together. The teacher who shows enthusiasm is much more likely to encourage his or her pupils to look, to find out and to assess.

The topics in this book should provide a basis for investigation, discussion and experimentation. Most of them can be used in any school and can be adapted to suit children of all abilities. Above all, the children should not only learn something about the world in which they live but also they should enjoy the processes by which they acquire this knowledge.

1 Living in water

The first plants and animals that appeared on the Earth lived in water. Of the millions of living organisms now in existence, a great many spend their whole lives in water, some of these living in the sea and some in fresh water. Although some schools do not have easy access to the sea and seashore, it is reasonably easy to find freshwater habitats — ponds, lakes, streams, rivers, ditches, canals, ornamental pools and even garden rainwater butts.

It may not always be possible for children to make a study of pond life, but it is important that they are given the opportunity to see how organisms have adapted to living in water. Even if it is necessary to take the 'pond' to them, it is well worth doing, and it is not difficult to set up some sort of aquarium in which specimens can be kept for a short time. Obviously, this is not as good as a visit to a pond or stream, but teachers working in the middle of towns may find such a visit is impractical.

GENERAL NOTES

Freshwater plants

1 Some flowering plants grow completely submerged and these show the greatest adaptation. They are unable to support themselves; instead they are supported by the water. All parts of these plants absorb water and the gases dissolved in it and there are no stomata ('breathing' pores). Some plants are rooted in shallow water, and have floating leaves. Others are completely free-floating. Both these types of water plants have stomata on the upper surfaces of their leaves through which air can enter.

Examples of flowering water plants include

a. *Totally submerged plants* — Canadian pondweed (Elodea), water milfoil
b. *Rooted plants with floating leaves* — water lilies
c. *Free-floating plants* — duckweeds, frogbit

Most water plants are perennials and are adapted to survive cold conditions. During the winter, some sink to the bottom of the pond where the water is warmer; the tops of some die back and new shoots appear next spring from the rhizomes buried in the mud; others form 'winter buds' which sink into the mud when the parent plant

dies, and these give rise to new plants the following year.
2 Most algae are found in water, the majority of species growing in the sea (seaweeds are algae). The largest group of freshwater algae is made up of green algae. Some of these are single-celled, while others are made up of groups of cells forming filaments. Examples of freshwater algae are

a. *Single-cell algae* — Diatoms (some are free-floating, others are attached to stones). A microscope is needed to see these attractive, tiny plants.
b. *Filamentous algae* — Spirogyra (found in floating masses in ponds).

3 The pond plants that can be found and studied include

Canadian pondweed (Elodea) — can be bought at aquatic suppliers.
Hornwort — easy to establish in a home-made pond, as it grows very quickly
Duckweeds — surface floaters
Water lilies — can be bought
Various algae.

Water animals
4 The animal life in and associated with fresh water is extensive, but a simple classification can be made and children can work from this. This classification could include

a. *Single-cell animals* — Amoeba, Paramecium.
b. *Multicellular animals*
   i. Invertebrates — Coelenterates (e.g., Hydra), worms and leeches, molluscs (e.g., water snails, mussels), arthropods (i.e. invertebrates with jointed limbs) (e.g., water shrimps, Daphnia, crayfish, insects — water beetles, dragonflies, mosquitos).
   ii. Vertebrates — fish (e.g., minnows, sticklebacks, perch), amphibians (e.g., frogs, toads, newts).

5 All fish live in water, absorbing oxygen through their gills. As water flows over the gills, oxygen passes into the blood stream. A fish has a streamlined body enabling it to move through water easily. Most fish are more or less the same shape, but there are exceptions (e.g., sea horses, flat fish — plaice).
6 Some animals spend only a part of their life cycle in water. Children ought to study the life cycle of at least one of the following examples so that they come to understand the meaning of metamorphosis.

Mosquito larvae (in water) → pupae (in water) → adult flying mosquito

Dragonfly nymph (in water for up to two years) → adult flying insect

Tadpole (in water) → frog (found on land and in water).

Note: Unlike the insect examples, the adults of both frogs and newts have to return to the water.

7 The pond animals that can be found and studied include

Amoeba and Hydra — need to be looked at under a microscope.
Snails — the great pond snail is the one most likely to be found. Snails can be bought quite easily.
Leeches
Water fleas (Daphnia) and water shrimps.
Water beetles and their larvae. Larvae of mayflies, mosquitos, damselflies, dragonflies and caddis flies
Adult frogs and newts, and their tadpoles
Fish.

ACTIVITIES AND EXPERIMENTS

Visit to a suitable pond or stream

1 If this can be organized, the children should be prepared for the visit, and taught the basic rules of conservation:

a. Plants around the pool or stream should not be damaged. Any specimens collected for further study should only be those indicated by the teacher.
b. If stones are moved, they should be put back in the same place and the same way up. Every stone provides a mini-habitat for some animal or plant.
c. Live animal specimens should be transferred carefully to suitable containers and should not be taken back to school unless they can be housed properly.
d. After specimens have been studied at school, they should be returned to the pool or stream where they were found.

2 The visit can be divided into

a. *Observation* — Are there any plants? Are they submerged or are their leaves floating on the surface? Are they free floating? Are there many plants? Do they grow in some areas only? Are there any animals visible? What are they? Are they on the surface, around the edge or swimming freely?
b. *Dipping* — Use fishing nets or kitchen sieves (under the supervision of an adult). Animals living in the weeds, around the edges and in the bottom mud can be caught and put into plastic containers to be looked at more closely.
c. *Recording* — Back at school, the pond can be charted to show

the distribution of plant and animal life. Each specimen can be identified and more found out about it by observation and using suitable reference books.

Developing a pond or aquarium

3 It is very worthwhile developing ponds at school (particularly if the school is in an area where a visit is extremely difficult) and these can vary from quite small to large, purpose-built ponds. These can be stocked after supervised visits to a pond or the stock can be provided by the teacher. The building of large ponds is not practical in most primary schools, but thick plastic sheeting can be used to line a hole dug in the ground. Small aquaria, plastic bowls and large sweet jars can be used as temporary ponds. As far as possible water and mud from the source pond should be used, but if it is necessary to use tap water it should stand for 24 hours before use. Examples of ponds that can be set up by the children include

a. Sweet jar with a layer of mud in the bottom and Canadian pondweed anchored into the mud with stones. This will house a few tadpoles and pond snails. (The surface area is small in relation to the water volume with the result that the water will not be well aerated without large quantities of pondweed so the number of specimens should be kept to a minimum.)

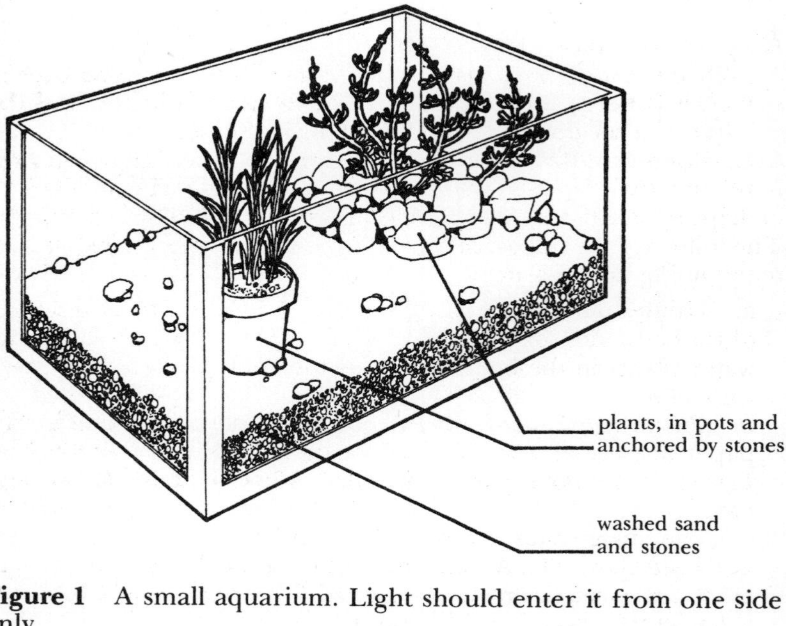

Figure 1 A small aquarium. Light should enter it from one side only.

b. A small aquarium, such as that shown in Figure 1, can be used to house fish, tadpoles (i.e. frogs and newts), snails, freshwater shrimps and several types of water plants. Algae will soon grow on the sides. These can be scraped off and be looked at under the microscope.

c. Large shallow plastic bowls can be used for floating plants and for those that root in the mud but have floating leaves. Although they cannot be kept in small containers for long, there will be sufficient time for the children to identify some of the characteristics of water plants.

Life cycles

4 Children are usually introduced to tadpoles at a very early age, but unless the tadpoles are housed and cared for properly they are not going to reach adulthood. Care should be taken to make sure that frogspawn is not removed from its natural habitat, except for a small clump of eggs for studying at school. A jamjar is not a suitable tank for tadpoles. Instead, they should be kept in tanks with plenty of waterweed and bottom mud collected from the same place. As it takes some time for tadpoles to change completely use can be made of films and slides to show this process of metamorphosis. Children can watch and keep records of the life cycle of a frog or newt. In addition, one of the water insects such as the mayfly should be studied.

Keeping and studying fish

5 While it is not always possible to catch fish that can be kept in school, it is quite easy to buy one or two small goldfish, and the children can set up a suitable aquarium for these.

Note: (Round goldfish bowls should never be used as the surface area in relation to the volume of water is too small.) If the fish are likely to be kept for some time, an aeration pump would be an advantage. The following are important points to consider when setting up and maintaining an aquarium.

a. Using a tank, sink or bowl, cover the bottom with a thick layer of washed sand, soil or pond mud. Put some stones on this. Plant water plants in the bottom layer or in small plant pots. Anchor with stones.

b. Put a large sheet of stiff paper over this and fill with water (the paper prevents the sand or soil being disturbed too much) (see Figure 2). Remove paper carefully. Allow to stand for several days.

c. Introduce snails and one or two fish.

d. Feed sparingly. A pinch of proprietary fish food given every other day is sufficient for two small fish. Remove any food not eaten as this soon fouls the water.

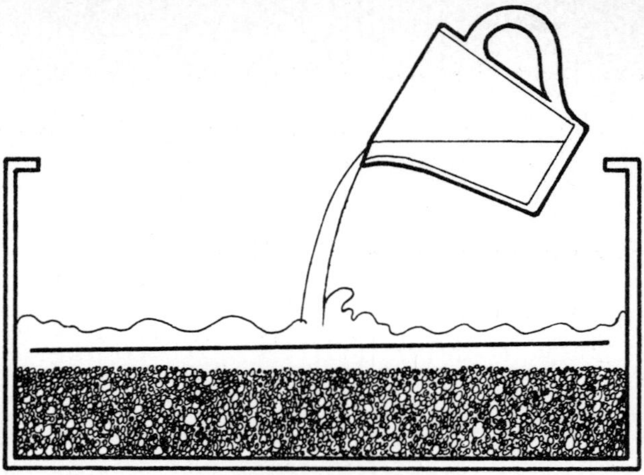

Figure 2 To avoid disturbing the soil, cover it with a sheet of stiff paper before filling the aquarium with water.

6 Children can look at movement (i.e. use of fins and tail), breathing and feeding.
7 In order to see the structure of a fish more clearly, the children can look at a fish such as a sprat or herring bought from the fishmongers. They should look at its overall shape, the position of fins (pectoral, pelvic, dorsal, ventral and tail), eyes (and absence of eyelids), mouth, gill covers and the gills under these. Scales can be looked at under the microscope or a good hand lens.
8 Water snails, which are easy to obtain and can be kept without much trouble, will help to keep the sides of the aquarium clear of algae. Groups of children could undertake detailed studies of these and other specimens as obtainable.

DEVELOPMENTS

1 A study of streamlining following a look at fish shapes and movement
2 Microscopic study of pond water
3 Water pollution and its implications
4 Fish farming and the life history of the salmon
5 Living in water — life in the sea
6 Looking at plant and animal life around rivers, ponds and lakes.

LINKS

1 See also **Size and shape** (Section 2) and **Seashore and cliff** (Section 18).
2 Environmental studies — conservation of ponds, distribution of such species as the common frog.

RESOURCES AND SUPPORT MATERIAL

Useful apparatus

Small aquaria, plastic bowls, fishing nets, kitchen sieves, plastic jars and boxes, hand lenses, microscope, thick plastic sheeting.

General reference books

Observer's Book of Pond Life J. Clegg (Warne).
A Guide to Freshwater Invertebrate Animals T. T. Macan (Longman).
Freshwater Life (Wayside and Woodland Series) J. Clegg (Warne).
A Handbook of Water Plants E. Bursche (Warne).

Children's books

The Pond Book J. Dyson (Puffin Books).
Freshwater Animals (Clue Books) G. Allen and J. Denslow (Oxford University Press).
The Seashore (New Naturalist Series) C. M. Yonge (Collins).
Learning about Insects and Small Animals R. Showell (Ladybird Books).
Pond Life (Living Science Series) K. Hutchinson (Macmillan Educational).
Frogs and Toads P. Clay and H. Clay (A. & C. Black).
An Aquarium R. H. C. Fice and I.M. Simkiss (E. J. Arnold).

Other resources

1 Save the Village Pond Campaign, 111 Lambeth Road, London S.E.1.
2 *Pond and River Birds* — (filmstrip) The Slide Centre (address see Section 21).
3 Set of pondlife charts by A. Leutscher (Macmillan Educational) (address see Section 21).

2 Size and shape

From a very young age, children are made aware of the wide variety of living things and they have, at various times, classified those that they know into various groups — birds, pets, trees, plants that we eat, farm animals, insects and many others. Gradually they can be introduced to more scientific classifications but first they need to grasp the idea that all living things are either plants or animals.

Obviously teaching the children complicated lists could be very boring and meaningless, but introducing them to even a limited range of plants and animals can give them some idea of the vast numbers of organisms living on Earth. Some aspects of variety can be shown by asking them to look first at shape and size.

GENERAL NOTES

1 If children want to classify living things (and many like doing this), they can start within a fairly simple framework as in Table 1.
2 Animals grow to a definite size and shape and once full size is reached they do not grow appreciably any more. Plants continue to grow throughout their lives, and have a less definite size and shape. Trees add to their girth annually and the rings formed can be used to find out the age of a felled tree.
3 The largest animal on Earth, and the largest animal that has ever lived, is the Blue Whale. It can weigh up to 120 tonnes — 40 times heavier than the largest elephant. It is a great deal larger than any of the prehistoric giant dinosaurs.

The largest plants are trees; the largest in the world is the Californian redwood, which can grow to a height of more than 112 m, and some are over 3000 years old.
4 Some plants and animals are so small that they can only be seen with a microscope, but children can see some tiny plants that are more familiar. (For example, the duckweed that grows on the top of ponds — each leaf is about 5 mm across.) One of the things that they can do is to find out for themselves facts about weight and measurements of many plants and animals. Children like doing this and will quite readily accept that an elephant has to be drawn smaller than life size, but an ant has to be drawn larger.
5 The largest animals live in the sea because of the support given by the water. This means that they do not have to have a skeleton

Table 1

Animals	**Plants**
A Invertebrates 1 Single-celled 2 Coelenterates 3 Worms 4 Crustaceans 5 Insects 6 Spiders 7 Molluscs ('shells') 8 Starfish and sea urchins	A Non-flowering plants 1 Single-celled 2 Algae 3 Mosses and Liverworts 4 Ferns 5 Cone bearing trees 6 Fungi
B Vertebrates *Cold blooded* 1 Fish 2 Amphibians 3 Reptiles *Warm blooded* 4 Birds 5 Mammals	B Flowering plants 1 Narrow leaved plants (monocotyledons): grasses, reeds, rushes, cereals 2 Broad leaved plants (dicotyledons): herbaceous plants, shrubs, deciduous trees
Examples Amoeba animal – invertebrate – singled celled. Cat animal – vertebrate – mammal.	*Examples* Oak plant – flowering – broad-leaved – deciduous tree. Mushroom plant – non-flowering – fungi.

strong enough to support their weight on land. A whale will die on land, although like all mammals it is an air breather, because its skeleton cannot support its great weight.

6 The shape of a plant or animal depends on its habitat and conditions of life. Examples

a. The streamlined shape of most fish assists them to move through water.
b. The frog has jointed limbs for moving on land and webbed feet for swimming.
c. The giraffe is adapted for feeding from foliage high up in trees.
d. The mole is shaped for burrowing and has powerful front limbs for digging.
e. Climbing plants do not need strong woody stems for support.
f. Water plants are shaped so that they float in or on water.

Children can find many more examples for themselves.

7 The limbs of animals need to support the weight of the body. The area of the foot needs to be broad enough to prevent the animal from sinking into the ground (e.g., look at the feet of the camel). A cow weighs about 400 kg so when the animal is standing still each leg has to support 100 kg. As the animal moves, the weight on each leg is increased, so the limbs have to be strong enough the support the animal — see also **Bones skeletons and movement** (Section 5).

8 Heat is lost from the surface of living organisms. Warm-blooded animals generate heat within their bodies and maintain a constant body temperature. Such animals must lose excess heat in warm conditions and retain heat in cold conditions. Cold-blooded animals absorb heat from their surroundings. If their body heat is too low, they become sluggish and some hibernate to conserve heat. Mammals and birds living in arctic regions tend to be large, but the smallest animals and birds in the world tend to live in hot climates. Larger animals living in hot conditions have to lose heat. An elephant, for example, has a small surface area compared with its weight. Areas of heat loss are increased by its floppy ears and folds of skin.

9 Plants absorb light energy to enable them to manufacture their food. Leaves have a large surface area to give them maximum exposure to light.

10 Measurements most commonly used when studying living things are

a. Length — of animals (i.e. from tip of nose to end of tail)
b. Height — of plants or standing animals (the height of a horse is measured from ground to shoulder)
c. Girth — of tree trunks, limbs of animals
d. Weight
e. Wing span — of birds, insects, bats
f. Volume — of water animals
g. Surface area — of leaves, whole animal.

ACTIVITIES AND EXPERIMENTS

Comparing animals

1 Give the children questions for which they have to find the answers. This could follow a visit to a zoo or seeing suitable films (e.g., *Life on Earth*). They will need a collection of good reference books. The following is a selection of possible questions.

What is the largest living animal? How big is it?
What is the smallest living animal? How big is it?
What is the smallest living mammal?
What is the largest (or smallest) mammal in Britain?
What is the smallest bird in the world?
What is the smallest plant that you know?
What is the tallest tree that you have seen? Where is it?

2 Measure and weigh animals so that the measurements can be compared. Children can weigh and measure fully grown animals — dog, cat, guinea pig, mouse and any others available. If possible they should follow the growth pattern of any small animal (e.g., a guinea pig) from birth to several months old. Human growth can be looked at if a parent can be persuaded to bring her new baby to school. The infant's development could be followed over six to twelve months. Children can compare the length of time it takes different animals to reach adulthood.
3 Children can undertake studies of specific animals so that they can assess their suitability for the environment in which they live. Taking as an example the domestic cat, several questions can be asked.

What is the average length and weight of an adult cat?
How old is a cat before it is fully grown?
How old is a cat before it can fend for itself?
Is the cat equipped for climbing, catching prey and defending itself against enemies?
How does it react to hot or cold weather conditions? What happens in wet weather?
What part does the tail play in movement?
Are its limbs suitable for its type of life?
What size are the feet? Can it walk over soft or muddy ground?

This could be followed by some work on the larger cats (e.g., lion, tiger) using film, slides and film strips to look at shape, size and movement.

Legs and weight support
4 Milk straws can be used to find out something about the weight that can be supported by an animal's limbs. If cylinders of plasticine are used to represent the animal's body, the milk straws can be used to represent the four legs. With a given weight of plasticine will the the legs support the weight if they are 5 cm, 10 cm, 15 cm or 20 cm long? Can the weight supported be increased if the straws are made into bundles of three, six or ten straws for each leg?

Surface area
5 A comparison of weight and surface area will show that area does not increase directly in proportion to weight. A mouse or guinea pig can be weighed, and a roll of paper, the same length and girth as the animal, can be used to find its approximate surface area. Older children can find the area-to-weight ratio by dividing the area by the weight. To find the approximate surface area of a child, cylinders of paper can be rolled round each limb, the head and the body. Added together these will give the approximate area of the body. How does

the area-to-weight ratio compare with that of the mouse or guinea pig?

6 If an A4 sheet of paper is folded in a zig-zag way, it can be seen that the paper now occupies a smaller space than it did when flat. This compares with the folds of skin seen on many of the larger mammals, giving them a greater area of skin for heat loss.

7 Children can look at the ways in which animals lose heat in hot weather. Some animals will cover themselves with water and lose heat by evaporation. (Children are often surprised that tigers will go into water in hot weather.) Dogs lose heat by evaporation of water when panting, and cats lose heat through their paws. Children can also look at the ways in which heat is retained by animals living in cold climates.

Note: With all these activities the amount of work that children can do is extensive; a great deal depends on the number of animals they can see.

DEVELOPMENTS

1 Animal and plant growth — speed of growth, life span.

2 Animals that change their shape and habitat during their life cycle (metamorphosis). Examples of these include butterflies and frogs.

3 Detailed study of a particular area to see how plants and animals are adapted for their habitat.

LINKS

1 See also **Bones, skeletons and movement** (Section 5) and **Living in water** (Section 1).

2 Mathematics — measurements and comparisons; estimates of weight, size and speed; graphs and charts of animal sizes; comparisons of speeds and sizes.

3 Geography — the Arctic and Antarctic and the animals of these areas, animals and plants of tropical areas.

RESOURCES AND SUPPORT MATERIAL

Useful apparatus

Balances, personal scales, tape measures, paper bags, good hand lenses, microscope, squared paper, plasticine, drinking straws.

General reference books

Life on Earth D. Attenborough (Collins).
Field Guide to the Mammals of Britain and Europe F. H. Van Den Brink (Collins).
Revised Nuffield Biology, Text 1: Introducing Living Things, Text 2: Living Things in Action (Longman).
Oxford Book of Flowerless Plants F. H. Brightman (Oxford University Press).

Children's books

Living Things R. Showell (Ladybird Books).
Woodland Life G. Mandahl-Barth (Blandford Press).

Other resources

1 Any zoo or natural history park.
2 Any natural history museum — Natural History Museum (address see Section 21).

3 Mathematics and nature

Most children are introduced, at some time, to various measurements based on the body and know how to measure a yard from the fingers of an outstretched arm to the tip of the nose. They may even know that Goliath, whose height according to the Bible was six cubits and a span, must have been a giant of a man (about 3 m tall).

Mathematically and historically, these are interesting facts, but there are many other aspects of mathematics and biology that will interest children and will be worth investigating. They will not only learn more about living organisms but they will also have to cope with some quite difficult calculations and mathematical concepts. This work can be adapted to almost any age and ability, and many of the problems can be made sufficiently difficult to stretch even the brightest child.

GENERAL NOTES

1 Historically length was measured using various parts of the body. Although an adult was originally used for these measurements children will realize very quickly how unsatisfactory they must have been. Examples include

Span — the length between the tip of the little finger and the tip of the thumb with the fingers fully extended

Foot — the length of the foot

Yard — distance between the tip of the nose and the fingers with the arm stretched out sideways

Fathom — length from finger tip to finger tip with the arms stretched out sideways

Hand — distance across the palm at the base of the fingers

Cubit — distance from the elbow to the end of the fingers

Inch — possibly the width of the ball of the thumb

2 Animals move in different ways and at different speeds. Facts about animal speeds can be looked up. Obviously it would be impossible for children to measure the speed of, say, a cheetah which can move at almost 113 kph, but they can measure the speeds of snails, woodlice and earwigs. The easiest way to do this is to let the animal move freely on a large sheet of paper for exactly one minute and mark its route. The line can then be measured and the speeds compared. For example

The woodlouse moved 114 cm in 1 minute
This would be 114 × 60 = 6840 cm (68.4 m) in 1 hour
Call this 68 m in 1 hour
Thus the speed is

$$\frac{68}{1000} = 0.068 \text{ kph}$$

Such calculations can be varied to find, say, the time taken to cover 1 m. Alternatively, graphs can be drawn to compare speeds or the distance moved in one minute.

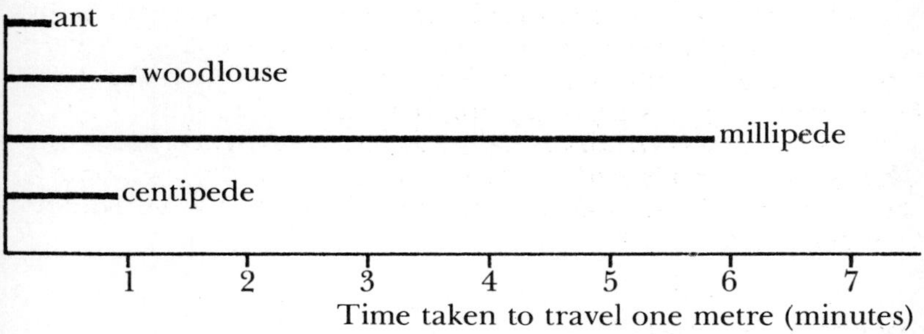

3 Spirals can be found in both plants and animals. For example, they can be seen in shells, the horns of some animals, climbing plants (stems and tendrils), the arrangement of leaves on stems, and in fir cones.

a. *Shells* — the spirals may be flat like the shell of the ramshorn snail or pointed like that of the whelk, garden snail or auger. If you hold the opening of a pointed shell towards you, you can see whether it spirals clockwise or anti-clockwise. The shells of these animals grow only at the open edge.

b. *Climbing plants* — some plants climb clockwise and some anti-clockwise. They do not vary. Children can try reversing the spiral by tying the plant's stem in the opposite way, but the plant will revert to its normal spiral. For example, convolvulus grows in an anti-clockwise — right-handed — spiral).

c. *Arrangement of leaves on stems* — look at a long twig of any plant. Start with one leaf and look for the next one, higher up, that is in the equivalent position. Count the number of turns, and the number of other leaves, between the two equivalent leaves. Tie a piece of thread to a leaf low on the stem and wind it round the stem touching each leaf as you go. It is then easy to see how many times it goes round between equivalent leaves. Consider the following example.

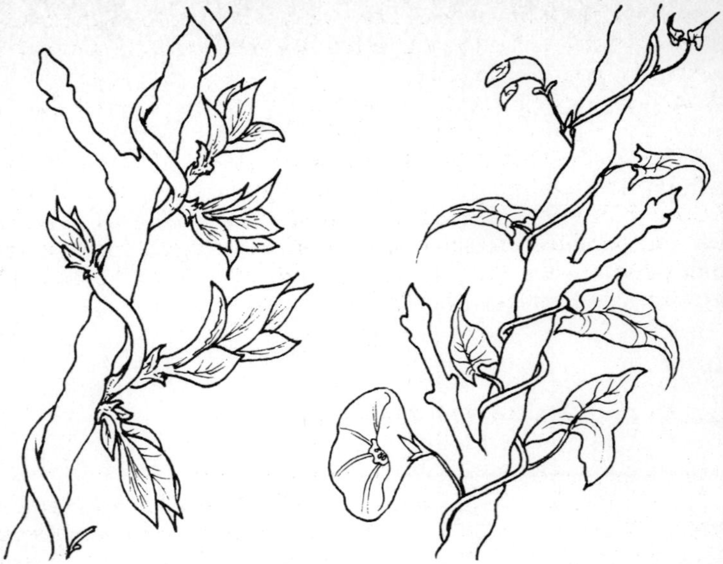

Figure 3 Two examples of plants that spiral as they grow, one clockwise, one anticlockwise. On the left: Honeysuckle. On the right: Convulvulus.

Hawthorn has four spaces between equivalent leaves, and the thread will spiral twice. Thus 2 turns and 4 spaces is $\frac{2}{4}$ so the ratio is $\frac{1}{2}$

These ratios can be compared so that the children can see if a definite pattern emerges. The leaves appear to be arranged so that each one gets sufficient light for photosynthesis.

4 Some shapes will tesselate — triangles, rectangles, squares, hexagons and shapes based on these. Children will probably have done some mathematical work on this. Honeycomb cells are hexagonal and although square cells would fit together equally well the following experiment will show that there are advantages if the cell is hexagonal.

The capacity of a triangular, a square and a hexagonal container, each with the same perimeter (say 18 cm) and of the same depth (say 4 cm), can be estimated by filling the boxes with sugar or sand (level the top with a knife).

5 Animals can, on the whole, be divided into two equal parts by one line of symmetry. This is easy to see when thinking about ourselves, but children find it quite difficult to see the line of symmetry in other animals. (The body of a cat can be divided into equal parts by 'cutting' the animal into two with a line drawn from the tip of the nose to the end of the tail.)

Many leaves are more or less symmetrical and some natural forms can be divided by more than one line of symmetry.

6 A limpet shell has to withstand the constant buffetting of sea and sand. It is domed and more or less triangular in shape. Both arches and triangles will increase the strength and stability of a structure. This can be shown in such structures as bridges, roofs, climbing frames and cranes. Models can be made to investigate these structures. See also **Stress, strain and structures** (Section 10).

ACTIVITIES AND EXPERIMENTS

Body measurements

1 Children can look at the use of the body as a basis for standard units of measurement and can decide how accurate these measurements are likely to be, and the importance of standard measures.

2 Once children have been taught to take their pulse rates, they can compare the increase in rate after various activities and can decide why this should alter.

Strength of materials

3 It is quite easy to collect bones (e.g., chicken and rabbit bones) and using the leg bones some work can be done on the strength of these. Using dowel, drinking straws, and paper tubes of approximately the same length and diameter as the bone, it is possible to determine whether or not the hollow bones are comparatively strong. If each sample is clamped to a table, weights can be hung on the free end until the breaking point is reached. The children will find that tubes are stronger than solid rods of the same weight and that bones are extremely strong.

Animal speeds

4 The rates at which animals travel can be compared, and children can make a chart of records — the fastest moving animal, the slowest moving animal, the fastest bird in flight, the fastest racehorse. They cannot measure these for themselves so they will have to use reference books.

5 The speeds of small animals (e.g., ants, earwigs, woodlice, centipedes, snails, caterpillars, beetles) can be measured either by the method described in the General Notes or by timing how long it takes the animal to move a set distance (say 25 cm). The trouble is that it is hard to get an animal to move in a straight line!

Growth

6 The rate of growth can be looked at. Pea or bean plants grown in pots can be measured weekly; plants grown in different conditions can be compared. Do pea plants grow more in hot or cold conditions, in sun or shade and in dry or wet conditions?

Shapes in nature

7 Children can collect examples of spirals in nature and can compare clockwise and anti-clockwise spirals. Which is the commonest? Plants spiralling in one direction (e.g., the clockwise spiral of the runner bean) can be tied in the opposite direction to see if they revert to the original spiral.

8 If some honeycomb can be obtained, the children can look at this and find out which shapes tesselate. By experimenting with boxes (see General Notes), they can try to find out why hexagonal cells appear to be best. As well as measuring capacity, they can also find out how many hexagons fit into a given area. Would it be possible to fit in the same number of triangles or rectangles of the same perimeter?

9 A great deal of work can be done on symmetry. Once children have understood what this means (by working with mirrors and paper models) they can look for symmetrical forms in nature. They can find those forms with one line of symmetry quite easily and will probably realize fairly quickly that nearly all animals are symmetrical (see Figure 4). Could a bird fly successfully if one wing was quite different from the other wing? If mammals had asymmetrical bodies would they face any difficulties (e.g. in walking)? They can look at an insect (e.g., butterfly, bee, wasp) and see how the animal

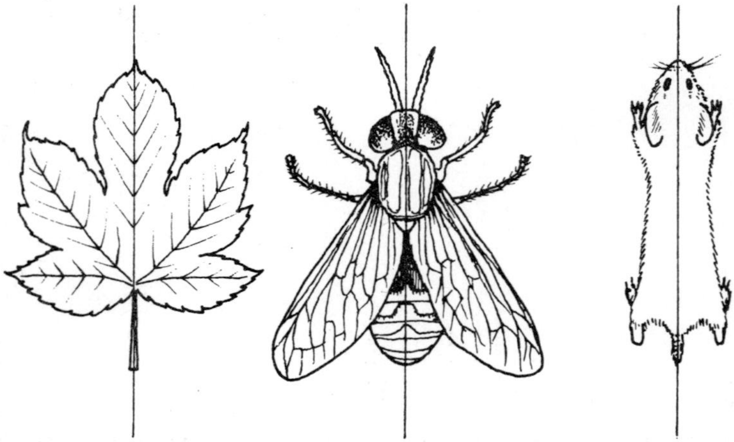

Figure 4 Lines of symmetry through a leaf, an insect and a mouse.

can be divided exactly by one line. Also they can investigate whether wings, veins, body markings and eyes are symmetrical.

Following this they can find examples of plants or animals with more than one line of symmetry.

Problem solving

10 Problem solving can provide children with opportunities for investigating both biology and mathematics. If the problems are well thought out, they will serve as excellent starters for more extended work.

a. A mouse can eat its own weight in food every day. Do you, or could you, do this? (If a mouse is weighed, a packet of food of the same weight can be shown. A child can also be weighed and food equal to his or her weight can be collected. *Note*: the smallest child in the class should be chosen for this experiment!)

b. What percentage of a packet of pea seeds will germinate? (If the children cannot cope with percentage they can find out how many seeds out of a given number will germinate.)

Can they decide what factors affect germination?

c. How much water is taken in by a plant in one day? (A glass jar can be used, with a cover made of strong polythene sheeting and a rubber band. A slit can be cut in this to introduce the root of a groundsel plant. Adhesive tape will reseal the slit. The water level at the start of the experiment and after one day can be marked on the jar.)

Will the plant take in most water if it is in the sun, the shade, the dark or a cool place?

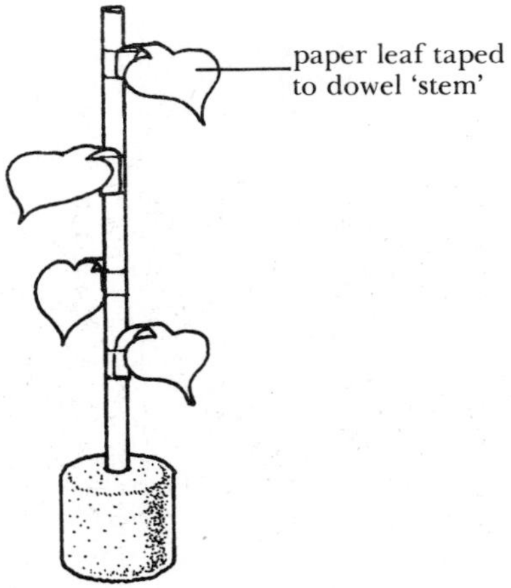

Figure 5 Recording the arrangement of leaves on a plant. A dowel stem supports paper leaves.

d. Do the shells of all pond snails, garden snails, whelks, etc. spiral in the same direction?
e. Are leaves all arranged on stems in the same way? (Models can be made by sticking thin dowel into a cork or a lump of modelling clay and then taping paper models of leaves onto this, copying the arrangement seen on actual twigs. This will show how leaves are positioned for maximum light, and the models can be used to show how the leaves spiral round the stem.)
f. How strong is a shell? (Limpet or mussel shells can be tested for strength if a piece of large, flat wood is put on top of the shell and weights are put on to this.)

Are all shells equally strong?

Are the shells of sea animals stronger than those of freshwater or land animals?

DEVELOPMENTS

1 Mathematical work on symmetry, tesselation, percentages, triangles, arches.
2 Work on the helix and the spiral — looking at springs, screws, spiral staircases, etc.
3 Ways different animals move. How shape and size affect the way an animal moves and the speed at which it moves.

LINKS

1 See also **Counting, sampling and solving** (Section 20) and **Bones, skeletons and movement** (Section 5).
2 History — the story of measurement.

RESOURCES AND SUPPORT MATERIAL

Useful apparatus

Seconds timers, corks, thin dowel, seed trays, plant pots, pea and bean seeds, mirrors, hand lenses.

General reference books

Using the Environment, 4: Ways and Means Science 5/13 Project (Macdonald Educational).
Life Size R. Gibbons and B. A. Blofield (Macmillan Educational).
Introduction to Biology D. G. Mackean (John Murray).
The Guinness Book of Records N. McWhirter (ed.) (Guinness Superlatives).

Children's books

Making Changes A. Wood (Macmillan Educational).

What is Symmetry? (Young Mathematician Books) (A. & C. Black).

Other resources

1 *LOOK! Primary Science Project* (Teachers' Guides and Pupil Cards) (Addison-Wesley).

4 Room to grow

If all mature seeds fell to the ground immediately below the parent plant, the result would be overcrowding. The increase in the competition for light, water and mineral nutrients would mean that far fewer plants would grow properly. New areas would not be colonized and species would not be distributed so widely.

Children can study the ways in which seeds are dispersed and they can also look at the features of plants which ensure that the seeds are carried away.

From a very early age, children may have collected fruits and seeds and watched willow-herb, dandelion, and sycamore drift in the air. Undoubtedly children find these objects fascinating because of the way they move, but there is much more work that they can do given the opportunity.

GENERAL NOTES

1 Many adaptations of plants enable seeds to be dispersed by either wind or animals. Some plants have explosive pods or capsules which propel the seeds away from the main plant, while others are adapted for water dispersal.

a. Wind dispersal

i. Fruits and seeds with 'parachutes' — willow-herb, dandelion, thistle, groundsel. These are light and easily moved by wind, often over very great distances.

ii. Winged fruits — lime, sycamore, ash. The wing-like structures cause the fruits to spin as they fall from the tree, and increase their chance of being caught in an air current and carried further away.

iii. Very light seeds — grasses.

iv. Swaying stems — poppy, campion, snapdragon. The ripe fruit capsule develops one or more holes, through which the small seeds escape as the long flower stem is moved by the wind.

b. Animal dispersal

i. Hooked fruits — burdock, goosegrass. The outsides of these

fruits have hook-like projections that catch on the fur of a passing animal.
ii. Birds carry fruits away to eat them and many of these must get dropped. Also some hard or waxy seeds pass through the digestive tract and are present in the birds' droppings.
iii. Most animals assist with dispersal. They may knock against plants or carry small seeds on their feet. The children seem to forget that even they are agents of dispersal, carrying and throwing such seeds as acorns and 'conkers'.

c. Explosive fruits — broom, lupin, gorse. The pods split suddenly and with sufficient force to expel the seeds. (On a hot day the pods of broom or gorse can be heard splitting open.)
d. Water is another possible agent of dispersal, and the interesting dispersal of coconuts can be discussed. Try to show them a coconut with the fibre covering still intact.

2 While children are introduced to the obvious ways in which seeds can be dispersed, there are many examples that cannot be fitted conveniently into one of the above categories. They should have the opportunity to see as many fruits and seeds as possible and should try to grow the examples that they find. Can they suggest ways in which such seeds as peas, broad beans, marrow, orange, apple and wheat are dispersed?
3 Some plants send out runners, producing new plants away from the parent (e.g, strawberry, couch-grass) This is the main method of reproduction, although the plants also produce seeds.

ACTIVITIES AND EXPERIMENTS

Collecting seeds

1 Children can make a collection of seeds arranging them into sets according to the more obvious methods of dispersal. Lids of shoe boxes covered with clingfilm make good display trays for these collections.
2 The sizes of seeds vary considerably. Can the children find out, by investigation, whether the method of dispersal has anything to do with the size of the seeds? Plants with large seeds appear to produce far fewer than those with small seeds. Is this true? Why should this happen?

Assessing types and efficiency of dispersal

3 If a tree (such as a sycamore) can be found growing more or less in isolation, the children can look for seedlings and estimate how far the fruits have been carried.

4 Look for plants growing in unusual places — in the guttering of houses, high up in a crack in a wall, in cracks in pavements — and try to decide how the seed reached these places.
5 Using sterilized potting compost, mix small quantities with the mud scraped off walking shoes, combings from a dog or cat, bird droppings (use an old spoon to collect these), dust swept off a path and brushings from a skirt or trousers after a walk in the country or a garden. If the pots are kept damp, children can see if any seeds germinate and, if possible, identify them.
6 As it is not easy to see ways in which seeds such as plum, peach, apple, pear, oak, beech and horse chestnut are dispersed, can the children think of any ways? Can they find out how commercial growers produce new plants? Can they find out more about the fruits and seeds of trees?

Wind dispersal

7 Experiments to see if some wind-dispersed seeds are moved more easily than others are best carried out on a fairly windy day. Children can release dandelion 'parachutes' and attempt to follow their progress. They can note the direction they travel in, how far they move, whether their speed varies, whether they travel in a straight line, and how long they remain in the air before sinking to the ground. Dandelion 'parachutes' can be compared with other fruits and seeds, such as willow-herb and groundsel.
8 The winged fruits of the sycamore can be released from different heights and their movement watched. Do they reach the ground quickly? How many times does a fruit spin round before reaching the ground? Does it move diagonally from the point where it is dropped? Would the seed move far from the parent plant?

Animal dispersal

9 If ripe poppy heads, with long stems are collected, they can be stuck into blobs of modelling clay. Using a hair drier as a wind source, experiments can be done to see how far the seeds are thrown out from the capsule.
10 As some seeds are adapted for clinging to animal fur, the children should collect fruits of burdock and goosegrass. They can test these on various materials — woollen cloth, cotton material, nylon stocking, sheep's wool, feathers or any others they can suggest — and decide which types of animals are most likely to be the carriers of these seeds.

Explosive seeds

11 If stems of lupin, gorse or broom are collected just as the pods are ripe, the children can measure the distance the seeds are thrown out of the pods as they split. Do all pods split when dry? Experiments

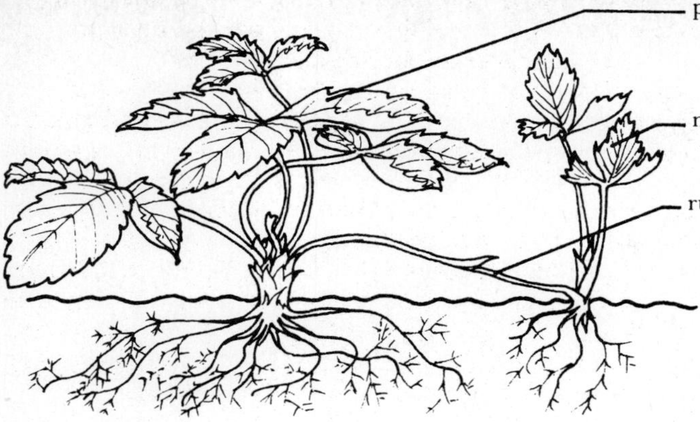

Figure 6 A new strawberry plant growing from a runner.

can be made with seeds of runner bean, broad bean, pea and vetch. (*Note*: Laburnum seeds are similar but are poisonous.)

Runners as a means of dispersal
12 Plants producing runners can be looked at (e.g., strawberry). The children can see how many runners are produced by one parent plant and how far away the new plants develop (see Figure 6). They can have a competition to see who can find the longest underground stem of couch-grass and can count the nodes with the new shoots, growing from the stem.

The importance of dispersal
13 Do plants need room to grow? What are the results of overcrowding? Looking at an old hedge, the children can see how all the plants grow so that their leaves obtain adequate light. Mustard seeds can be planted in two pots of soil with the seeds scattered sparingly on the top of the soil in one and covering the soil thickly in the other. If both pots are kept watered and placed in a warm light place, the development of the plants can be compared

DEVELOPMENTS

1 A more detailed study of vegetative reproduction.
2 Growth and development of seeds.
3 Growing various seeds, particularly those that the children find for themselves in gardens, parks, fields, hedgerows, woods and streets.
4 Growing tree seeds. Larger seeds such as acorns and 'conkers'

can be grown on top of bottles. If these are soaked for 24 hours and then put on top of a narrow-necked bottle so that they just touch the water their growth can be watched. Other seeds can be planted in potting compost.

5 A detailed study can be made of a particular area and the dispersal of plants can be looked at. If possible, areas can be compared. Do all plants grow in all areas? Will, for example, willow-herb grow anywhere? Will the seeds that germinate in a woodland area also germinate on moorland or open cliff top?

6 Reproduction of flowerless plants — ferns, moulds, fungi.

LINKS

1 See also **Exploring your environment** (Section 19).

2 Geography — plants in the tropical rain forests.

RESOURCES AND SUPPORT MATERIAL

Useful apparatus

Tape measures, hair drier, plant pots, potting compost, hand lenses, small boxes and trays for collections, cling film, seconds timer, modelling clay, plastic bags for collecting.

General reference books

Introduction to Biology D. G. Mackean (John Murray).
Using the Environment, 3:Tackling Problems Science 5/13 (Macdonald Educational).
The Oxford Book of Flowerless Plants F. Brightman (Oxford University Press).

Children's books

The Puffin Book of Gardening M. Kelly (Penguin Books).
Crops We Grow R. H. C. Fice and I. M. Simkiss (E. J. Arnold).
Flowers in the Garden E. Wrigley (Dinosaur Publications).

Other resources

1 Wild flower seeds — Thompson and Morgan (address see Section 21).

2 Set of tree charts — Philip Harris Ltd (address see Section 21). Staffordshire.

3 Information about trees — The Forestry Commission, (address see Section 21).

4 Any garden centre for small plant pots, potting compost, seeds and gardening tools.

5 Filmstrips — The Slide Centre, Philip Harris and Ladybird Publications (addresses see Section 21).

5 Bones, skeletons an[d] movement

Children like bones and skeletons; they are synonymous with creepy stories and the mock horror found in comics. This fascination can be used to get them interested in the bony framework of the body, and the general structure and movement of vertebrates (i.e. animals with backbones).

Many children seem to think that only man has a skeleton and are often quite surprised when it is pointed out that cats, dogs, horses, goldfish, frogs and tortoises have skeletons too. In fact, all the mammals — from the tiniest mouse to the massive blue whale — birds, fish, reptiles and amphibians are vertebrates.

GENERAL NOTES

1 The skeleton is the bony framework supporting the softer parts of the body (see Figure 7). The muscles attached to it enable the body to move. Movable connections between bones are called joints. The skeleton also protects — the skull protects the brain and the rib cage protects the heart and lungs.

Most vertebrate skeletons are made of bone, a hard substance composed mainly of calcium compounds. Many bones are tubes, so they are light but comparatively strong. The soft inner tissue (the marrow) manufactures red blood cells. The ends of some bones are covered with a softer substance (cartilage) which eases movement. The skeletons of sharks and some other related fish (e.g., skate and dogfish) are composed of cartilage.

2 The human skeleton consists of 208 bones ranging from the tiny bones of the ear (the ossicles) to the largest bone — the femur or thigh bone.

The backbone (vertebral column) is made up of 33 separate bones called vertebrae. Apart from the five lower vertebrae (called the sacrum) which are fused together, these are separated by cartilage and attached to each other by ligaments. The spinal cord runs through a channel in the vertebrae. The skull is made up of several bones fused together and immovable; only the lower jaw can move. The 12 pairs of ribs, with the breast bone (sternum) and thoracic vertebrae, form a cage containing the heart and lungs. The collar bones (clavicles) and shoulder blades (scapulae) provide attachment for muscles and support the arms. The hip girdle (pelvis) is a ring of strong bones, partly enclosing and protecting the organs of the lower abdomen. The legs are attached to the pelvis.

Obviously children will not remember the names of all the bones but they like using these and can be introduced to the correct names while they are talking about the skeleton. For example

Backbone — vertebral column — made up of vertebrae
Upper arm bone — humerus
Lower arm bones — radius and ulna
Thigh bone — femur
Lower leg bones — tibia and fibula
Hip girdle — pelvis.

3 Some bones are joined together but there is no movement between them (e.g., the bones of the skull), while others are connected loosely so that movement is possible. Bones meeting at a movable joint are covered, at the point of contact, with cartilage and connected by ligaments. The amount of movement varies according to the type of joint.

a. *Ball-and-socket joints* (e.g., femur and pelvis at the hip joint, humerus and scapula at the shoulder joint) allow considerable movement.
b. *Hinge joints* (e.g., the elbow) allow backwards and forwards movement.
c. *Pivot joints* (e.g., the skull pivoting on the first vertebra) allow turning.
d. *Gliding joints* (e.g., in the ankle and between vertebrae) allow limited movement.

4 All movements of the body are caused by muscles, thus much of the body tissue is muscular. Muscles vary in size from the tiny muscles moving the eye to the strong, large thigh muscles. Some muscles can be moved at will (e.g., moving the arm or leg, turning the head, bending the back). Others work automatically (e.g., those in the intestine). The heart is a strong, muscular pump that beats continually.

5 Although all mammals have basically the same skeletal structure, there are many adaptations, and children can find many examples for themselves.

Humans walk upright on the hindlimbs, other animals walk on all four limbs.

The limb bones of seals have become flippers for swimming.

The neck vertebrae of giraffes have become elongated, so that the animal can feed on high foliage (n.b. giraffes have the same number of neck vertebrae as humans).

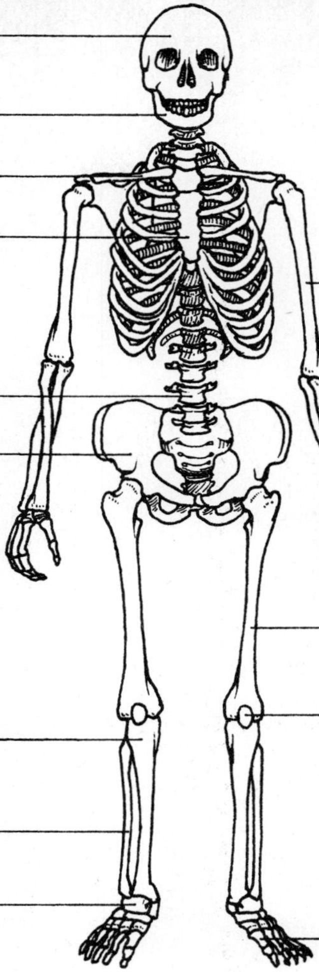

Figure 7 The human skeleton.

Hoofed animals do not have separate toes.
The wings of bats have evolved from the forelimbs (see Figure 8).

Reptiles, birds and amphibia can be seen to be similar. Fish have no obvious limbs and are adapted for movement in water.

6 Some invertebrate animals have hard exoskeletons which protect the inner, soft parts of the body. Crabs and lobsters are obvious examples, and insects have hard, chitinous outer coverings.

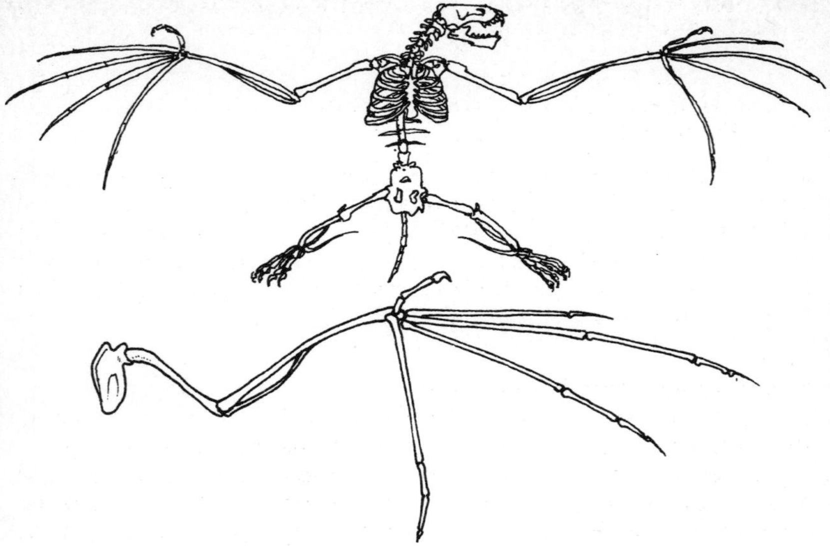

Figure 8 The skeleton of a bat, showing the 'arm bones' which have adapted to support wings.

A tortoise has a hard outer shell but is a vertebrate, the shell being formed from some of the vertebrae.

7 Bone is a living tissue. If it is broken, new bone grows to repair the break.

ACTIVITIES AND EXPERIMENTS

Identifying and comparing bones

1 Bones are not difficult to collect. They are frequently found on beaches and moors, and in fields, gardens and parks. While it is not easy to identify the animal to which they belong, it is usually possible to name the type of bone. Bones from chickens, rabbits and fish can be collected from the kitchen. (Boil poultry or rabbit bones in detergent and dry them in the oven.) Children can make the collections, labelling the bones that they know and, if possible, comparing them. The vertebrae from a rabbit can be compared with those from sheep; the size will differ but the structure is basically the same. If children find the vertebrae with two small holes, in addition to the central canal, they will know that they have neck vertebrae.

Owl pellets often contain the tiny bones of field mice, and individual bones can be picked out using tweezers and a hand lens.

2 Depending on what bones the children can find, various other investigations can be carried out.

a. Sorting bones by shape.
b. Comparing skulls of small animals.
c. Finding the weight of bones.

3 The children could visit to a museum to see the bones of prehistoric animals. (These will be fossilized bones.)
4 With a partner, the children can identify the position of the bones of their own bodies and can try to answer questions. Where is the largest bone in the body? How many bones are there in each finger? Why are so many bones necessary in each hand?

Structure and function of bones
5 A large bone — bought from the butcher — can be cut across to show the strong outer bone and the soft marrow in the centre.
6 Bones have to be strong enough to support the animal, but light enough for it to move about. Many of the bones are tubes, and some experiments can be done to test the strength of tubes. If a long bone from the leg of a chicken or rabbit is used with similar shaped pieces of pencil, dowel or rolled up card they can be clamped to a table so that most of the length overhangs. Weights can be hung on one end, using the nylon nets in which oranges and other fruits are bought, until breaking point is reached. The children will find that bones are extremely strong in relation to their weight, and they can discuss the importance of this.
7 Making different movements, the children can decide which joints they are using. Ask them to perform the following movements.

a. Sit down and stand up again.
b. Pick up a pencil.
c. Turn the head as far as possible.
d. Walk up some steps.

8 A visit to a zoo can be used to look at the shapes of as many animals as possible and to see how the skeleton affects movement.

a. A horse moves on its single-toed feet.
b. Most mammals have a tail, which is an extension of the backbone. Which animals use their tails? How do they use them?
c. The teeth in the skull vary. Do the type of teeth give an indication of the animal's food?
d. Snakes have more than a hundred vertebrae. The joints between these are very flexible.
e. Fish have skull bones and vertebrae, but their other bones are very different from those of mammals.

DEVELOPMENTS

1 A study of movement and speed of movement.
2 Streamlining and movement in air and water.
3 A look at some of the invertebrates.
4 Teeth and food.

LINKS

1 See also **Size and shape** (Section 2).
2 History — the use of animal bones as agricultural or hunting implements.
3 Geography — distribution of animals throughout the world.

RESOURCES AND SUPPORT MATERIAL

Useful apparatus
Tape measures, boxes for collections, cling film, small G-clamps, hand lenses.

General reference books
Illustrated Biology B. S. Beckett (Oxford University Press).
The Skeleton and Movement B. R. Ward (Franklin Watts).
Introduction to Biology D. G. Mackean (John Murray).
Movement in Animals D. Reid and P. Booth (Heinemann Educational Books).

Children's books
Bones (Clue Books) G. Allen and J. Denslow (Oxford University Press).
Living Things R. Showell (Ladybird Books).

Other resources
1 A museum with a natural history department.
2 Set of overhead projector transparencies, for example, *The Skeleton* — Audio-Visual Productions.
3 *Skeletons* set of 35 mm slides showing bones and skulls of various animals — Audio-Visual Productions.
4 Miniature skeleton — Philip Harris Ltd (address see Section 21).

6 Invertebrates and a snail study

It is not always easy to convince children that biologically the word animal applies to *all* living organisms that are not plants. They usually assume that only mammals and reptiles are animals. It is only by constant reference and by showing them examples that they will come to understand that such things as flies, snails, woodlice, beetles, minnows, sparrows and shrimps are also animals.

Having looked at some of the vertebrate animals, they can be introduced to the invertebrates. Many of these are the familiar 'creepy crawlies' that they already know so well and that are reasonably easy to collect. Such a study may also overcome some of the prejudices that colour the children's attitudes to many of the small animals. Why do they show interest in a snail but are repelled by a slug? An earwig will be stepped on because it is 'nasty' but a ladybird is picked up, and those fascinating animals the spiders seem to be regarded as particularly repulsive!

GENERAL NOTES

1 Invertebrate animals — meaning those having no internal skeleton — are found everywhere. It is not easy to make a simple classification but Table 2 should be helpful.

2 Many invertebrate animals can be kept by the children so that they can watch the growth and development for themselves. They should be shown how to keep each animal in a suitable container and how to feed it properly. This will not only ensure that the animal survives but will also teach children a respect for the living things they find around them.

a. Caterpillars can be kept in a large plastic sweet jar, with a piece of net and a rubber band for a lid. The food plant, inside this jar, will keep fresh if its stems are put in water in a small pot. It is important that the correct plant is used as food, so any child finding a caterpillar should note the plant on which it was found. As some caterpillars pupate in soil, a layer of damp peat can be put in the bottom of the jar.

b. Earwigs, woodlice and millipedes can be kept in a shallow box with a lid made of muslin or net. Damp leaves, a piece of inverted

Table 2

Type of animal	Characteristics
1 Single-celled animals	Very small animals living in water. Most can only be seen with a microscope. They are very abundant.
2 Multicellular animals	
a. Coelenterates	Hollow-bodied animals, such as sea anemones, jellyfish and hydra.
b. Flatworms	Mostly freshwater animals.
c. Worms	Include the familiar earthworm, and the ragworms and lugworms found near the sea.
d. Arthropods	
i Crustaceans	Crustaceans have hard exoskeletons like the insects. Those that the children will know are the crabs, lobsters and shrimps.
ii Insects	Insects have six legs, and most have one or two pairs of wings. The largest group of living things on Earth.
iii Spiders	Spiders have eight legs and no wings. Not all spiders spin webs.
e. Molluscs	Includes all the 'shells' (i.e. snails, cockles, oysters) and the squid and octopus.
f. Echinoderms	A group of sea animals, including starfish, sea urchins and sea cucumbers.

turf and a few small stones should also be included in the box, which is best made of tin, wood or plastic.

c. Spiders are not difficult to keep provided that they are fed properly. A suitable cage is shown in Figure 9 (this can also be used for caterpillars). So that any webs are left intact, they can be fed with small live flies through the feeding hole in the lid. They also need drops of water.

3 Snails belong to the class of animals called the gastropods. They have a muscular foot and a coiled shell into which they can withdraw. Because of the spiral growth of the shell, it can grow longer as the snail matures, the direction of coiling always being the same for a given species. When looking at a snail, the children will also be able to see the two pairs of tentacles with the eye spots at the end of the longer pair, and the hole in the foot, near the edge of the shell, through which the snail breathes. If a snail is put on a piece of glass or perspex and viewed from beneath, the muscular movement of the foot can be seen, as well as the mouth opening. Snails secrete a

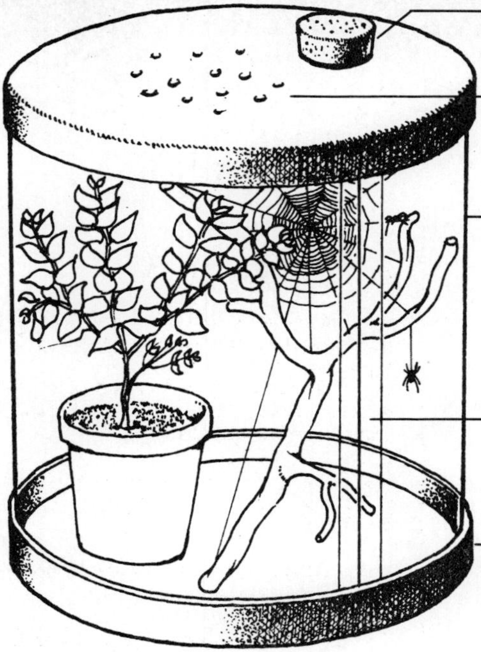

Figure 9 A cage suitable for spiders or caterpillars.

sticky mucus which helps them move over any surface.

4 Snails are hermaphrodites — each snail being both male and female. When they mate sperm is transferred from each snail to the other, and after mating, the snails lay eggs. The garden snail lays clutches of 20–30 eggs in damp soil. They are round, soft and semi-transparent, and usually hatch in about six weeks. Newly hatched snails are like miniature adults, and they reach maturity in about one year.

5 The garden snail feeds on vegetable matter and can be heard feeding because of its method of scraping leaves with its rasp-like tongue.

6 If children are going to undertake a reasonably detailed study of snails, they will need a good reference book to help them with identification (see the list of books at the end of the section).

ACTIVITIES AND EXPERIMENTS

Keeping snails

1 The best way for children to learn about garden snails is to keep them. The children could make a suitable cage using a large wooden box, an aquarium or an old washing-up bowl, with a fine-mesh netting lid as shown in Figure 10. Put a good layer of damp soil on the bottom of the container and arrange some stones so that the snails can get under or between them. Keep the cage in a fairly cool, shaded place and feed the snails daily with fresh green leaves. Remove any that are left uneaten or they will rot and become smelly. As snails do most of their feeding at night see that they have fresh food in the evenings. If they are given some rolled oats, the droppings will be less messy and easier to remove from the cage. A little powdered chalk added to the oats provides the necessary calcium for shell formation. If the soil is kept moist, there is a good chance that the snails will lay eggs. The children can look for these and, once the young snails have hatched, can keep notes of their development. (*Note*: Snails hibernate in winter in sheltered cracks and crannies. They withdraw into their shells, sealing the opening with dried slime.)

Movement

2 How fast do snails move? The children can find this out — see **Mathematics and nature** (Section 3) — and they can also find out if snails can move across all types of surface. Snails cannot move if they become too dry, so surfaces need to be slightly damp.

3 If snails are found outside, the shells can be marked with a dab of paint or nail varnish and an attempt made to plot their travels over 24 hours. If a snail is removed from the place where it was found and put a short distance away, does it return to the place where it was originally found?

Distribution

4 If there is the opportunity to study a particular area, the children can count the number of snails seen each day. If they want to make a count over a week, the snails seen should be marked with a small dab of paint or nail varnish so that they can see if the population alters. This work could be further divided by counting the numbers of different types of snails found.

5 Measurements can be taken of snails found — length of foot, width of shell. Is there a variation of size in apparently fully grown snails? If one snail is kept in a jar for a short time the amount of food eaten can be estimated. (A similar series of activities could be carried out with pond snails.)

6 If the school is in an area where land snails are reasonably easy to find, a study could be made of the spirals of the shells. Are there more snails with clockwise spiralling than with anti-clockwise spiralling shells? Do all snails (pond and sea snails included) have spiralling shells?

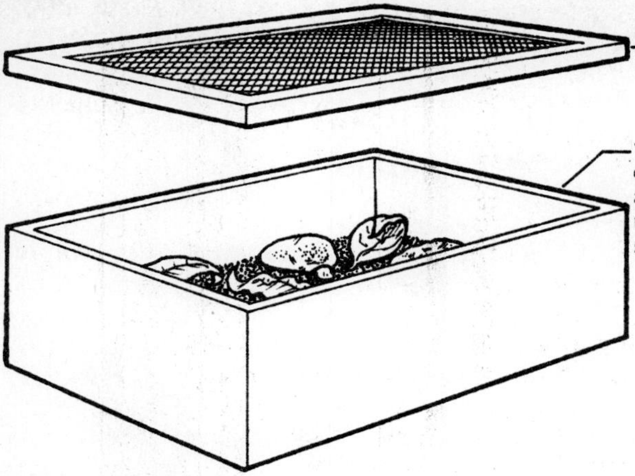

Figure 10 A cage suitable for snails.

Effect of stimuli

7 Do snails react in any way to various stimuli? Children can devise experiments to see their responses to different stimuli.

a. Do snails prefer dark or light?
b. Do snails like a warm or a cold surface?
c. Will they move through an area where there are hanging wool or cotton threads?
d. Will they instinctively move towards food?

DEVELOPMENTS

1 Undertaking a fuller study of land and water snails.
2 Further work on hibernating animals and factors affecting hibernation.
3 Finding out more about molluscs (this animal phylum, *Mollusca*, has about 80 000 species and includes all the 'shells'). Children will be able to find out that most of the molluscs are sea-dwelling animals.
4 A look at the other small animals likely to inhabit a garden — slugs, earwigs, millipedes, woodlice, earthworms and any others the children can find.

LINKS

1 See also **Mathematics and nature** (Section 3) and **Seashore and cliff** (Section 18).

2 Mathematics — speeds, spirals, size.
3 Looking at other spirals found in nature and man-made spirals such as springs, screws and spiral pathways.

RESOURCES AND SUPPORT MATERIAL

Useful apparatus

Large plastic boxes, plastic sweet jars, small aquaria, minute timer, sheet of glass or perspex, paint or nail varnish.

General reference books

A Field Guide to the Land Snails of Britain and N.W. Europe M. P. Kerney (Collins).
School Projects in Natural History Devon Trust for Nature Conservation (Heineman Educational Books).
Minibeasts Science 5/13 (Macdonald Educational).

Children's books

Learning about Insects and Small Animals R. Showell (Ladybird Books).
The Oxford Book of Invertebrates D. Nichols and J. Cooke (Oxford University Press) — not an easy text but excellent illustrations.
Woodland Life G. Mandahl-Barth (Blandford).
Science Workshop, 1 I. Finch (Longman).

Other resources

1 Simple balance for weighing snails and other small animals — Philip Harris Ltd (address see Section 21).
2 Callipers for measuring small animals — Philip Harris Ltd (address see Section 21).
3 *Animals of Leaf Litter* (set of 24 slides) — Philip Harris Ltd (address see Section 21).
4 *Learning about Insects and Other Small Animals* (filmstrip) — (Ladybird Publications).

7 Reactions — how plants respond to stimuli

A child knows that if he puts his hand on something hot or sharp he will feel pain and move his hand away very quickly. He also knows that a cat will react strongly if its tail is trodden on. He accepts that animals have 'feelings' and that they will respond in some way, but the responses of plants to stimuli are not so obvious. While the necessity to move away from danger can be seen in the various ways in which animals react, the movements of plants are far slower and it takes longer for the child to realize that these movements are essential to plant growth and development.

GENERAL NOTES

1 Plants cannot move from place to place, but they can alter their direction of growth. These growth movements, which are the responses to stimuli, are called tropisms. The tropic response to light is called phototropism; to gravity, geotropism; and to water, hydrotropism. These responses ensure that the plant has sufficient water and that the leaves are positioned in such a way that they get enough light for the manufacture of food (i.e. photosynthesis). The response to gravity means that the root will grow downward and the shoot will grow upward. Tropic responses can be positive or negative. For example, leaves growing towards the light show positive phototropism, but they also show negative geotropism (i.e. growing upwards against the pull of gravity).

2 Tropisms also enable a plant to adapt to changing or adverse conditions. For example, a bulb, when planted upside down, will grow so that the roots curve downwards and the shoot upwards. Similarly, if one water source dries up, the roots can alter direction to grow towards another available source.

a. Phototropism is not always obvious in plants growing outdoors because light is usually evenly distributed, but plants growing in very crowded conditions tend to have tall, straight stems as the plants grow upwards towards sunlight. A potted plant growing in a room with only one window has leaves that not only grow towards the window but also are angled so that the maximum light reaches the leaves.

b. Geotropism is a growth movement in response to the pull of the Earth's gravity. Roots need to grow down into the soil to obtain mineral salts and water, and to anchor the plant in the ground. The shoot reacts negatively to the pull of gravity, and so grows upwards through the soil into the light.
c. A root tends to grow towards a source of water (positive hydrotropism). This can be seen where trees are growing alongside a pool or stream. The roots grow into the bank and are often exposed when water washes the soil away.

ACTIVITIES AND EXPERIMENTS

Phototropism

1 The children can put potted plants (e.g., geraniums) on a window sill and leave these, without turning the pots, for several days. The leaves will grow towards the light source. If the pots are then turned round, the leaves will slowly change their direction so that they are again leaning towards the light.
2 Pea or bean seedlings can be grown in pots until the leaves are well developed, and they can then be put into a box with a slit cut in one side only so that the light reaching the plant is from one point only. The plants will grow towards the slit and, if left long enough, will grow out through it. The children need to be reminded that they must not turn the plants round when they water them.

Geotropism

3 Using a strong cardboard box, the children can make a potato maze. A hole is cut at one end of the box and the children then build barriers inside using thin card and leaving a space first at one side and then at the other side. If a shooting potato is put at the end, away from the hole, and the lid is put on, the shoot will eventually grow round the barriers and out through the hole.
4 Mustard seedlings can be used to show the response to gravity. For this the children need two sheets of perspex, strong rubber bands and cotton wool. A thick pad of cotton wool is put on one sheet of perspex and thoroughly dampened. A few mustard seeds which have previously been soaked are put on the cotton wool and the other piece of perspex is placed over the top and secured with the rubber bands, making a 'sandwich' which is stood on its edge. Once the seedlings have produced good roots, the sandwich can be reversed so that the roots are pointing upwards. For this experiment it is important that the cotton wool is kept moist all over and is not left standing in water (or it will be difficult to decide if the roots grow down in response to gravity or water).
5 By cutting a cork in half and scooping out a small groove, a pea

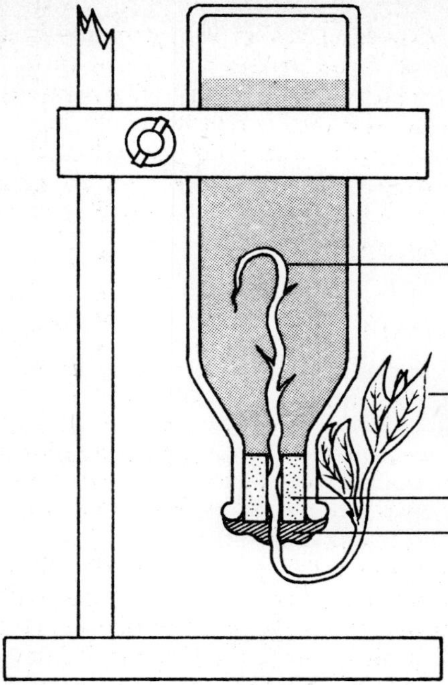

Figure 11 Demonstrating a plant's response to gravity. When the plant is inverted, its roots and shoot change their direction of growth.

seedling can be grown in a bottle. The cork is put round the stem of the seedling, and the root is introduced into a bottle of water, with the shoot growing upwards. To make the cork waterproof, drip some melted candle wax on to it or press modelling clay over it and round the stem. Once the plant is growing well, turn the bottle upside down and fix it to a stand. Gradually, both the root and the shoot will reverse their direction of growth as shown in Figure 11.

Hydrotropism

6 To show the response of roots to water, grow pea or bean seedlings on wire netting or in a sieve so that the netting and soaked seeds just touch the water. Once good roots have grown down into the water lift the netting off and cover the seedlings with damp peat or cotton wool. Keep this damp and the roots will curve upwards towards the new source of water.

Problem solving

7 After trying out various simple experiments, children can devise some for themselves to answer problems set for them.

a. What happens if the shoot of a plant is kept in the dark?
b. Will leaves react to artificial light as well as natural light?
c. Do all plant leaves react to light?
d. Do all plant roots react to gravity? What about plants growing in cracks of walls or similar places?
e. Do water plants react in the same way as land plants?
f. Plants grow in deserts where water is very scarce. How are their roots adapted for taking in water?

DEVELOPMENTS

1 Looking at the reactions of animals to stimuli, particularly those reactions necessary for escaping from danger.
2 Looking at plant growth in various geographical regions — deserts, arctic regions, tropical forests and swamplands.

LINKS

1 See also **Room to grow** (Section 4).
2 Mathematics — measuring the speed of response in a plant (e.g., the time taken for a leaf to grow towards a source of light).
3 Environmental studies — growth of trees planted for timber (i.e. those growing straight, with tall stems in the case of conifers).

RESOURCES AND SUPPORT MATERIAL

Useful apparatus
Plant pots, peat, cotton wool, perspex sheets, small trowels, corks, glass bottles, black paper, growing plants, pea, bean and mustard seeds, strong cardboard boxes, adhesive tape.

General reference books
General Science, Book 2 C. Windridge (Schofield and Sims).
Illustrated Biology B. S. Beckett (Oxford University Press).

Children's books
Plants and How They Grow F. E. Newing and R. Boxwood (Ladybird Books).
Stems M. Clarke (Hart-Davis Educational).
Plants M. Edwards (Evans Brothers).

Other resources
1 *Plants and How they Grow* (filmstrip) — Ladybird Publications.

2 Any garden centre for plants and seeds, small flower pots and trowels.
3 *Plants* (chart pack) — Macmillan Educational (address see Section 21).

8 The next generation

One of the characteristics that distinguishes living organisms from those that are dead or non-living is their ability to reproduce. Without this there would be no continuity of life, and even the youngest children readily appreciate that plants and animals are capable of producing new offspring. They will also understand that although some non-living things, such as cars and aeroplanes, can move freely and need fuel to keep them running they are not able to reproduce themselves and so cannot be alive.

Children find the whole subject fascinating, and they ought to be introduced to the biology of reproduction from the earliest years. It is a pity that, even at this age, the whole subject is too often referred to as sex education, when all that is being offered is a fairly simple biological study. Sex education comes later when children are more able to realize the social and moral implications of sexual behaviour.

GENERAL NOTES

1 Living organisms produce offspring that are eventually like themselves although some do not always look like the parents in the early stages. Examples include

Tadpole → frog
Caterpillar → moth or butterfly

2 Sexual reproduction involves the union of male and female cells. Most living organisms reproduce sexually. Seeds are the product of sexual reproduction in plants.

3 Most animals reproduce themselves by producing eggs which are fertilized and develop into young animals. Fertilization is the fusion of the female cells (the ova) and the male cells (the sperm). In mammals, fertilization occurs within the female's body where the embryo develops, the period of gestation differing from animal to animal. Most other animals lay eggs, with the young developing inside the egg after it is laid. In some animals, fertilization is external, the male shedding sperm over the eggs after the female has laid them (e.g., amphibians and most fishes). Animals that are born in nests tend to be less developed than those born in the open. The latter need to be able to move away from predators from the moment of birth.

4 Children are more familiar with reproduction in mammals than they are with that in other animals. They probably have a cat or dog at home and they may have pet rabbits, guinea pigs or hamsters. They may also realize that they belong to this group of animals. In mammals, which are usually covered with fur or hair and are always warm blooded and vertebrate, the young develop inside the mother. After birth, they are fed with milk from mammary glands.

5 Plants usually produce seeds in large numbers thus ensuring that each species of plant will continue. Flowers are pollinated (the pollen carries the male cells) in various ways — by wind, by insects, by self-pollination — and once the seeds are formed the flowers wither and die. A seed contains all the elements necessary for development and growth into a mature plant resembling the parent plant. The tiny seeds of a poppy will grow into new poppy plants and acorns will grow into oak trees.

6 Asexual reproduction does not involve two individuals. In its simplest form, the organism divides into two (e.g., the amoeba — a single-cell freshwater animal). Vegetative reproduction in plants is asexual. Many plants can be reproduced both vegetatively and from seeds. Examples of vegetative reproduction include

a. Bulb — daffodil and tulip
b. Corm — crocus
c. Stem tuber — potato
d. Root tuber — dahlia
e. Runner — strawberry

Gardeners make use of the ability of plants to reproduce in this way when they divide large clumps of plants, take cuttings from leaves or twigs, or graft such plants as roses and apples.

ACTIVITIES AND EXPERIMENTS

Sexual reproduction in animals

1 Children can best watch the growth and reproduction of a mammal by keeping animals such as guinea pigs. These attractive, small animals produce their young after a gestation of about ten weeks, and as these are so well-developed they can be handled carefully within a few hours of birth. This means that the children can weigh them and note their rates of growth from birth to maturity. Any animals kept at school must be kept in ideal conditions — cages should be dry, roomy and draught-proof — and provision has to be made for weekends and holidays. A suitable cage for mice is shown in Figure 12. The children need to be taught how to clean out and feed the animals. If the animals are kept at school and there is a male and a female, the whole process of breeding can be watched

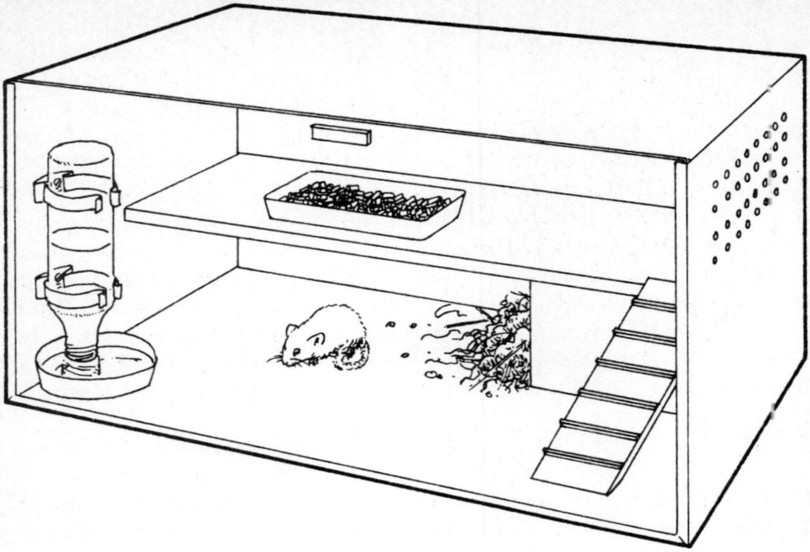

Figure 12 A cage suitable for mice.

from mating to the birth and growth of the baby animals. The group caring for the animals could write a book of instructions, to be passed on to the next group.

2 Children can keep other small animals and watch their growth — see **Invertebrates and a snail study** (Section 6). If fish are kept at school, the children can find out more about breeding them.

3 Other animals (e.g., a cat with kittens, a dog with puppies) can be brought to school for a short time so that the children can compare the young animals with the adults. After they have seen these familiar animals they can find out more about other animals and record the following details.

a. Name of the animal
b. Gestation period (e.g. cat — 63 days, cow — 282 days, horse — 340 days)
c. Number of young normally born
d. Development at birth
e. Amount of parental care
f. Age when animal is capable of fending for itself
g. Age of maturity
h. Life span.

4 A visit to a zoo or bird sanctuary in the spring to see baby animals would be useful.

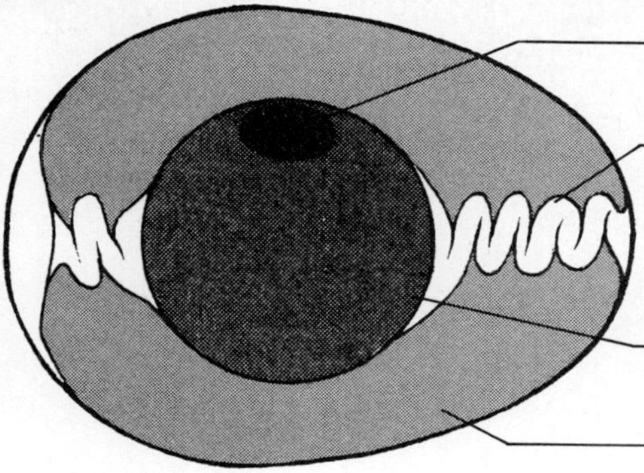

Figure 13 A cross-sectional view through a fertilized hen's egg.

5 Following a visit to a zoo or after seeing an animal film or filmstrip, the children can find the answer to such questions as

a. Do large mammals always have proportionately large babies?
b. Other than humans, do parent mammals teach their offspring in any way?
c. Are all cats (i.e. domestic, lions, tigers) born helpless and with their eyes closed for some days after birth?
d. Do small mammals tend to give birth to numerous babies at one time?
e. Does the size of the adult mammal or its young have anything to do with the length of gestation?

6 Make a collection of pictures or drawings showing parent animals with offspring that are completely unlike them in the early stages.

7 Look at a hen's egg as an example of a bird's egg (see Figure 13). Even though the chances are that this will be unfertilized, the children can see the general structure of an egg.

a. How is the growing baby bird protected?
b. On what does the unhatched bird feed?
c. How does a baby bird break through the shell and hatch out of it?

Find out about the eggs of other animals (e.g., reptiles, amphibians, fish, snails and insects). How are these protected and do egg-laying parents look after their offspring? How long does the embryo take to develop before hatching?

The children can find out as much as possible about eggs and can write about them.

Sexual reproduction in plants

8 Children can collect seeds and try growing them in potting compost. Seeds such as orange, grapefruit, apple and pear need to be dried first. While plum, peach and apricot seeds will grow, they take a very long time to germinate; the very hard outer coverings have to rot first but if these are cracked carefully, it may speed up germination. Fruits and seeds that can be collected from almost anywhere include willow-herb, dandelion, groundsel, thistle, ragwort, grass, shepherd's purse, foxglove and buttercup. They can try growing any that they find.

9 In order to watch germination more closely large seeds such as beans and peas can be grown and the following questions answered.

a. Which part of the plant grows first?
b. How long does the seed take to germinate?
c. How long is it before leaves appear?

Vegetative reproduction in plants

10 Plants can be grown vegetatively. If twigs of weeping willow are put into a bottle of water, roots will appear on the lower parts of the twigs. Does this happen with twigs from other plants? If the work is begun in the winter, cuttings from pot plants can be used. The children can also try growing new plants from leaves, pieces of stem and pieces of root. Mint is an easy plant to use for experiments.

Family trees

11 The children can make family trees of their own family, but the teacher needs to use considerable tact where he or she knows that there are children from one-parent families, a child is adopted, or where the natural parents have been divorced or separated. If there is any doubt about this topic, the teacher can choose one family (getting the assistance of the parents involved).

Heredity

12 Do children always take after their parents? If the mother and father are both tall will all their children be tall? Does hair and eye colouration vary between brothers and sisters?

DEVELOPMENTS

1 A study of growth and development of animals and plants.
2 Animal families — looking at the family as a unit.
3 Characteristics of living organisms.
4 Development of the human embryo and the birth of a baby.

LINKS

1 See also **Room to grow** (Section 4) and **Invertebrates and a snail study** (Section 6).
2 Mathematics — gestation periods, comparing birth size with size of the adult, speed of development, comparing the size of animals with such factors as life span and age of maturity.
3 Geography — animals of the world and different breeding habits according to the natural habitat of the animal (e.g., life cycle of the salmon, birth of some bears during the period of hibernation in the coldest part of the year, turtles and places where their eggs are laid, animals born in a very undeveloped state that continue their growth in a pouch — i.e. marsupials).

RESOURCES AND SUPPORT MATERIAL

Useful apparatus

Appropriate animal cages, scales with deep pans for weighing small animals, plant pots, potting compost.

General reference books

Introduction to Biology D. G. Mackean (John Murray).
Keeping Animals in Schools Department of Education and Science (Her Majesty's Stationery Office).
Minibeasts Science 5/13 (Macdonald Educational).

Children's books

Introducing Science, 2 S. Jackson (Blackie).
How You Began H. Spiers (Dent).
A Baby in Our Family Althea (Dinosaur Publications).
Plants and How They Grow F. E. Newing and R. Boxwood (Ladybird Books).
Living Things R. Showell (Ladybird Books).

Other resources

1 *Starting Life* (series of four film strips with audio casette — *Seeds and Babies*, *Mammals and Their Families*, *Families from Eggs*, *Families with Backbones*) — VP Educational Resources (address see Section 21).
2 *The Keeping of Animals and Plants in School* (Leaflet 11), *Living Amphibians as Classroom Animals* (Leaflet 23) — School Natural Science Society (address see Section 21).
3 *Merry Go Round* (three films — *Beginnings*, *Birth*, *Full Circle*) — B.B.C.
4 Moth and butterfly eggs and caterpillars — The Butterfly Farm

Ltd, Bilsington, Nr. Ashford, Kent and World Wide Butterflies Ltd (address see Section 21).
5 *Life Cycle of a Plant* (filmstrip) — Hugh Baddeley Productions (address see Section 21).

9 Friction and movement

There is a great deal of practical work involving tools, machines and movement that children can do. They probably already know something about wheels and simple pulleys, and they will have played with toys that roll and bounce, or are moved by some sort of motor. Without realizing it, they will also have met the effects of friction — when they use the brakes on their bicycles, when a drawer will not pull out easily or when a match is struck on the rough side of a matchbox. Because it is a feature of everyday life, there are many easily controlled experiments that children can do to find out more about movement and resistance.

GENERAL NOTES

1 Friction is a force producing resistance when two objects move over or against each other. The rougher the surfaces the greater the friction. Even apparently smooth surfaces may have very small projections inhibiting movement.
2 Friction can cause damage when surfaces rub together and the heat produced can, in some circumstances, cause serious problems. Some machine tools have to be cooled continuously to prevent the damaging effects of the heat produced by friction.
3 Friction can be overcome by using very smooth surfaces, lubricants, wheels, bearings, rollers and air streams (i.e. the hovercraft). Lubricants separate two surfaces so that projections cannot catch against each other. For example, a stiff hinge responds spectacularly when oiled.
4 Friction can be used to slow down movement and to give grip. Without friction it would be impossible to walk about. Also, it is used in braking and in non-slipping belts on machinery. The tread on tyres provides a grip for the moving vehicle.

Machines and animals moving on land must get a grip on the surface over which they are moving. Animals have feet that are adapted for their own environment. For example, the polar bear has broad feet, furred on the underside for walking on smooth surfaces, and a cat, with its sharp claws, is less likely to slip on a polished floor than a dog. We wear suitable shoes according to what we are going to do; running, playing tennis, climbing, driving and so on. Floors can be treated to produce maximum friction (i.e. non-slip surfaces).

5 Resistance preventing movement (e.g. when a parked car's handbrake is on) is called static friction. When there is movement, but with resistance, it is called sliding friction. The force preventing the movement of an object so that it does not move at all is greater than that resisting the movement of something in motion.
6 Another result of rubbing two surfaces together can be abrasion. This occurs when wood is sandpapered to rub away a rough surface, and when an abrasive cleaner is used on, say, a dirty saucepan.

ACTIVITIES AND EXPERIMENTS

Looking at friction

1 Make two friction boards with pieces of wood planking (at least 1 m × 20 cm) — one should be as smooth as possible and the other can be left rough. Get the children to rub the smoothest with fine sandpaper and then polish it with good wax polish. The boards can be propped up — making steep slopes — against any suitable object. (A pile of bricks is useful as the slope can be altered easily by adding or taking away bricks.) After the children have experimented by sliding different objects down both slopes, they should be able to see that a smooth object moves reasonably easily down the smooth slope and that the poorest result is obtained using a rough object on the rough slope.

Having done this they can undertake more controlled experiments by using objects of the same size and weight, but with differing surface finishes, on each board. Matchboxes filled with clay or plasticine can be used to produce uniform blocks, and different materials (e.g., sandpaper, plastic, rubber, paper, various fabrics or anything that the children can suggest) can be stuck on the bottom surfaces. Using the same apparatus, the children can also find out if weight and size affect the results.

Friction and force

2 Using a smooth, horizontal surface, get the children to pull a wooden block (with a screw eye for attachment) across the surface with a strong rubber band. The stretch of the band will indicate the amount of force needed to move the block. Different materials can be attached to the underside to see the effect on the force needed to move the block. The block must be started in the same place each time, and the children will need to devise a means of measuring the amount of stretch. Older children can use a spring balance.

Overcoming friction

3 The apparatus used in both the previous experiments can be used to find out if lubricants will overcome friction. Children can experiment with such things as butter, water, oil, grease and soap. (*Note*: The friction boards and other surfaces will need to be cleaned in between experiments using a detergent of some sort.)

Friction and heat

4 Children can produce heat using friction by rubbing their hands together, but they will probably say that this is simply body heat. The bowl of a tablespoon can be rubbed vigorously on a mat or carpet; the heat produced can be felt if the spoon is put against the inside of the wrist.

Wheels, bearings and rollers

5 Using one of the pieces of planking previously described as a slope (not too steep), toy cars with their wheels fixed either by adhesive tape or by rubber bands can be pushed down it. The angle of the slope can be altered until the toy cars move. The children will see that the cars will remain still on a slight incline and that they will only move easily when the wheels are freed. Experiments with different sized wheels and other models can be included here.

6 Get the children to put several bricks in a stout box (preferably a strong, wooden one) and then try to push it across the playground using one finger only. They can be asked to think of ways of making this easy and can be introduced to the idea of using rollers (made from broom handles). Alternatively, if the box is large enough, a child can sit in it and other children can be asked to find the best way of moving the load across the playground.

7 Place a shallow tin lid on the floor with the inner surface downward and ask a child to stand on it with one foot and try to twist the tin round. After putting several marbles or ball-bearings under the lid ask the child to try again. (Make sure that another child is holding his or her hand when this is done.) A similar experiment can also be done using two paint tins; fill each with sand, stack one on top of the other and try to twist the top one round using one finger. This cannot be done unless ball-bearings are put between the two tins.

Floors and footwear

8 A pair of old shoes or plimsols can have the bottoms covered with grease and a child can be asked to try to climb a sloped board while wearing them. (This can lead to a study of suitable footwear for different activities, following a discussion on the importance of friction for getting a firm grip on surfaces.)

9 Is a floor safe? A study of the floors at school could be undetaken by a group, and they could look at potentially dangerous places (e.g., where food could be spilled, where water is spilled or where the floor is over-polished). The importance of high friction can be stressed.

10 The legal specification for tyre treads can be looked at. Ways of testing the safety of tyres can be devised using pieces of rubber (preferably pieces cut from an old tyre). These can be tested on rough, smooth, wet, dry and oily surfaces.

Machinery

11 Study of a bicycle, looking at the tyres and brakes (using friction) and places where oil is necessary to overcome friction. The children can then look at other items including machines and tools that may require oiling (e.g., scissors, pliers, door and window hinges, swings, moving toys) and can oil them if needed. They could also draw up a set of rules for the care of equipment.

Friction where we least expect it

12 Get the children to look around and to find where we meet friction everyday. They can decide whether it is an advantage or disadvantage. Examples include striking a match, writing, moving furniture and drawing curtains.

Abrasion

13 Give the children fairly rough pieces of wood and ask them to make the surfaces as smooth as possible. If they are supplied with various materials (e.g., cloth, paper, plastic, leather, sandpaper, etc.), they can try them all. They may also think of rubbing the wood on rough ground.

14 An old saucepan can be burnt deliberately (i.e. by boiling milk in it and letting it boil dry) and the children can try cleaning it with soap, detergent, commercial abrasive cleaner and sand.

DEVELOPMENTS

1 Finding out more about lubricants, particularly oil.

2 Testing graphite as a lubricant— using crushed pencil lead. (Is it true that pencil rubbed up and down a metal zip makes it move more easily?)

3 Investigation of the force needed to start an object moving and the force needed to keep it moving.

LINKS

1 Mathematics — movement and speed following work on brakes. (Are the brakes likely to be less effective when a vehicle is moving at speed? What are the shortest stopping distances at different speeds?)

2 History — the history of the wheel, the use of rollers to move heavy objects (e.g. they were probably used to move the stones at Stonehenge).

3 Model making — making a model trolley or other toy with some sort of braking system.

RESOURCES AND SUPPORT MATERIAL

Useful apparatus

Wooden planks (1 m × 20 cm), bricks, wooden blocks, screw eyes, strong rubber bands, matchboxes, plasticine, string, wheeled toys or roller skates, sandpaper, fabrics, plastic sheeting, rubber sheeting and rubber pieces, spring balance, broom handles, marbles or ball bearings, tin lids, wooden boxes, pieces of wood (and a saw for cutting), adhesive tape, lubricating oil, grease, proprietary abrasive cleaner.

General reference books

Look! Primary Science Teachers' Guide, B C. Gilbert and P. Matthew (Addison-Wesley).
Exploration for Young Scientists, B. J. K. Tricker (Mills & Boon).
General Science, 3 C. Windridge (Schofield and Sims).
General Science, 5 C. Windridge (Schofield and Sims).

Children's books

The story of Oil R. Unstead (ed.) (A. & C. Black).
Bicycles A. Dixon and D. Sheasham (A. & C. Black).

Other resources

1 Construction toys.
2 Wheeled toys.
3 A bicycle.

10 Stress, strain and structures

From the moment an infant begins to place one brick or beaker on top of another and tries to build something, he is involved with structures. When the whole thing falls over because the bricks have not been placed correctly, he is starting to learn something about the construction of bridges and buildings. As the child gets older he will see around him examples of girders and frames, of arches and towers, of different types of bridges and of such things as cranes and scaffolding. Everywhere he looks he will see man-made structures. All of these have had to be constructed from suitable materials and in such a way that they are appropriate for their particular uses.

All children like building things, so something about structures is likely to appeal to any age group.

GENERAL NOTES

1 When any material is compressed or pulled by equally opposing forces, it is under stress. Stresses cause materials to bend or, if too strong, to break. Tubing will stand greater stress than flat strips, so a bicycle frame is made of metal tubing.

2 The change of shape of a material caused by stresses is called strain. When structures are being designed, the effects of all the forces they will be subjected to have to be allowed for; the materials used have to be strong enough to withstand them. The strain caused by two equal forces pushing together is compression while that caused by those tending to pull apart is tension.

3 Many structures (e.g., bridges, cranes) have the framework joined in such a way that triangles are formed — rectangular shapes collapse easily under stress, but triangular shapes are much stronger. This can be seen very easily using simple models.

4 With an arch, the load is distributed so that it is carried by the sides of the supports, but there is a tendency to push outwards. With large arch bridges, this is overcome by building abutments at either end; these need to be large and heavy enough to counteract the outward thrust.

5 Bridges are of four main types:

a. The *beam bridge*, in its simplest form, is a plank laid across a stream and, therefore, supported only at each end. A long, flat bridge has a tendency to bend in the middle and if the stress is too great the bridge could break. To overcome this beam bridges are often built with several supports, reducing the length of any section (e.g., the Britannia Bridge over the Menai Straits in North Wales).

b. The *arch bridge*, in its modern concrete form, is seen over many motorways. A very famous arch bridge is the Sydney Harbour Bridge in Australia.

c. The *cantilever bridge* is made of two beams, each supported at one end. The Forth Railway Bridge in Scotland is an example of a large cantilever bridge.

d. The *suspension bridge* consists basically of a track supported by cables slung between the two ends. Very primitive suspension bridges made of rope have been used for hundreds of years, but a modern bridge has steel cables slung between towers. They are stronger than they look, although there can be considerable movement. The Clifton Suspension Bridge, Bristol, will move as much as 30 cm up and down in a high wind.

There are many bridges that are variations of the main types. Quite a lot of work with the children can involve looking at bridges, or pictures of them, and trying to decide what type of bridge each one is. (*Note*: Tower Bridge, London has cantilevered arms which can move up and down.)

6 Walls are worth studying on their own. This sort of work can be carried out in the country or in a city centre. Walls can be of historical interest or very new, but there are various things that the children can look at

a. The purpose of the wall
b. Material used for building
c. Method of building
d. Associated plants

For more information on a possible study, see *Teaching Science to Infants* R. Showell (Ward Lock Educational).

7 Buildings and other structures make use of many different materials. Again, this could form the basis of a group or class project. Examples of different types of materials include

a. Natural stone — either used as it is found or shaped in some way. This includes slate, an important roofing material in the past, but not used so much these days.

b. Bricks — manufactured stones, cuboid in shape but of many different types

c. Concrete and mortar

d. Metal — steel girders and frameworks, reinforced concrete, window frames

e. Wood
f. Other materials — plastics, glass, plaster, cement, putty, paint.

ACTIVITIES AND EXPERIMENTS

Constructions

1 Using drinking straws all sorts of structures can be made (these can be joined using soft wire). If the children want to make larger structures they can use tubes made out of sheets of newspaper. (If six or more pages are rolled up tightly and then rolled in a further sheet that has been pasted all over, the result, when dry, will be a firm tube of paper.) Can the children make a structure that will test the strength of such tubes? Using newspaper tubes is it possible to make a structure that will support a child?

Strength of triangles

2 Using wooden, metal or plastic strips join four pieces to form a rectangle. This can be pushed out of shape quite easily, but if another piece is added — so that it forms a diagonal and makes two triangles — the shape remains rigid. This is a very simple model, more complicated ones can be made; the children will devise these for themselves if given the materials. Old metal Meccano is ideal, but plastic will do almost as well.

3 If three bamboo poles are joined at the top so that a tripod is produced, the children will find that it collapses if they lean on it, but if they make a triangular base (with a leg attached to each angle) the structure is then extremely rigid and will withstand a lot of pressure (see Figure 14).

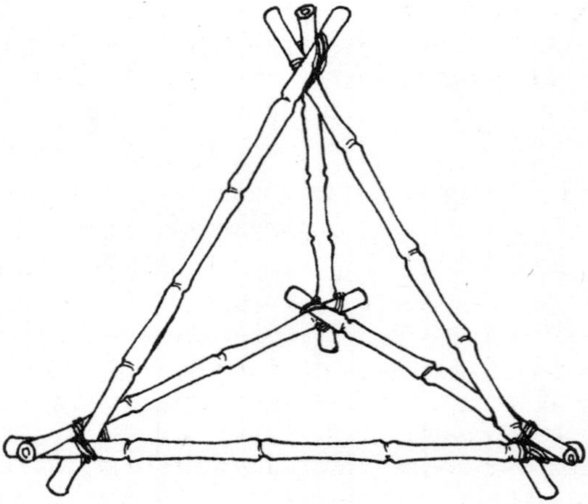

Figure 14

4 Make a collection of structures using triangles (i.e. drawings, pictures, models and photographs).

Bridge building

5 Using bricks, pieces of wood, boxes and strong card, models of bridges will give the children a good idea of structure. These should be made strong enough to take heavy toy cars or trucks.

a. A simple beam bridge can be built using three match boxes for each end support and a card roadway. If the card is more than a few centimetres long it will bend in the middle when a toy car is put on it. This can be counteracted by adding an additional support in the middle, or by bracing it with struts that form triangles.

b. The bridge made from the single strip of card can be compared with one made from a curved piece of card (forming an arch). This will have to be fastened at each end with drawing pins. If weights are put on both bridges, it will be seen that the arch is the stronger.

c. Experiments can be performed using Meccano. Various bridges can be made and the strength tested. Ways of strengthening the structures can be devised. How can the bridge be made rigid without adding a cumbersome amount of metal?

d. It is not easy to make a model arched bridge from bricks (made from clay using small boxes as moulds) and having a keystone, but this is possible and the children can experiment until they find the best way of doing this.

e. A model suspension bridge can be made by suspending a board from ropes slung between two chair backs.

Breaking stress

6 Test the breaking stress of various materials by clamping one end to a table and hanging weights on the other. The weights can be put in a large can with a wire handle attached. Test wood, plastic and metal rods and strips. Are strips or rods stronger? Is a tube stronger than a solid bar?

7 If children have done the previous experiment, they will have found out that tubes are proportionately stronger than other structures of approximately the same size. Various tubes — of the same length but of different diameters — can be rested on two bricks and weights hung from the centres of the tubes to determine if the diameter of a tube makes any difference to its strength. If the tubes are stood on end and weights are placed on them, the vertical strength can be estimated.

8 If children are to understand that strength does not depend only on size they need to do some work on the shape of the building units used in a structure. If they are given several strips of card (approximately 30 cm × 10 cm) they can test the strength if these are folded length-wise in various ways. If they look at some real girders they can get some idea of the ways in which metal strips are used.

Materials

9 Several experiments can be carried out to compare the properties of different materials.

a. Find out the difference between cement, concrete and mortar.

b. If possible the children can test different mixes of concrete (a mixture of sand, cement and gravel). This can be done by casting small beams in a mould and testing them in the same way as they tested tubes. (Concrete for beams is normally one part cement, two parts sand and four parts gravel mixed with enough water to make a stiff consistency).

c. Model bricks can be made with clay cast in matchboxes and different brick bonds can be tried when building model walls. Which are the strongest?

DEVELOPMENTS

1 Buildings and waterproofing.
2 Tools and machines used for building.
3 Road making.
4 Interesting and unusual structures — cranes, transporter bridges, drilling rigs, domes.
5 Looking at other building materials such as paint and plastics.

LINKS

1 See also **Metals all around** (Section 13) and **Sticking it together** (Section 15).
2 Geography — bridges around the world.
3 History — castles, history of buildings, the story of road building, bridge building.
4 Mathematics — triangles and structures, geodesic domes, arches and curves, study of bending stress and breaking stress.

RESOURCES AND SUPPORT MATERIAL

Useful apparatus

Plastic and metal meccano, any constructional toys, toy cars and trucks, builders' bricks, string, rope, soft wire, stiff card, plywood strips, drinking straws, newspapers, glue.

General reference books
Structures and Forces Science 5/13 (Macdonald Educational).
Elements of Structure W. Morgan (Pitman).
Looking Around in Town and Country P. Sauvain (Franklin Watts).

Children's books
Bridges R. Loxley (Ladybird Books).

Other resources
Structures Science Pack — E. J. Arnold and Son.

11 Keeping warm and keeping cool

It is quite obvious that temperature changes according to the season; it is colder in winter than it is in summer. Children realize that although it is fun to play in the snow they will need warmer clothes than they needed in the sunshine of August! In the winter, homes and schools have to be heated, but in summer it can be so warm that, even with all the doors and windows open, the temperature is too high for comfort.

By looking at the ways in which we, and other animals, keep warm or keep cool, children can begin to understand more about insulation, and reflection, absorption and conduction of heat.

GENERAL NOTES

1 Dark, dull surfaces are good absorbers of heat, but light, shiny surfaces absorb very little. Black polythene sheeting, used by gardeners to cover such things as strawberry beds, absorbs available heat and warms the soil underneath.
2 Bright, shiny surfaces reflect heat. Electric fires often have bright metal surfaces behind the source of heat, so that the heat is reflected into the room. In hot countries houses painted white keep cooler because heat is reflected and not absorbed. Similarly, light clothes tend to be cooler than dark ones.
3 Heat is passed through matter by conduction. If we want to prevent heat loss we need to use bad conductors (i.e. insulators). Metals are very good conductors of heat so a saucepan with a solid metal handle will get too hot to pick up. If it has a wooden or plastic handle (i.e. a poor heat conductor) it can be used safely.
4 Air is a very poor conductor of heat, so loose materials which contain trapped air will keep the heat in. Examples are

a. A bird's feathers — in very cold weather the bird fluffs out its feathers so that the layers of air trapped act as an insulator, preventing some heat loss.
b. Woollen clothes — these are warmer because of the air trapped between the fibres. If clothing is loose the layer of air between the clothing and the skin also acts as an insulator, keeping the body heat in.

c. Expanded polystyrene and fibreglass — these are used to insulate lofts and cavity walls to stop the heat of the house being lost. These insulators also help to keep the house cooler in very hot weather when the sun is beating down on the roof.
d. Double-glazed windows — these keep heat in because the layer of air between the panes of glass acts as an insulator.

5 Cool clothes are thin (i.e. little air is trapped between the fibres) and light-coloured (to reflect heat and not absorb it) and leave areas of skin exposed so that sweat evaporates quickly. (Evaporation causes cooling of the skin.) Obviously in very sunny conditions the skin has to be covered to prevent burning.

6 Mammals and birds are warm-blooded and maintain a constant body temperature so they need to be able to retain heat in cold conditions and to lose heat in hot conditions. Several examples of adaptations exist.

a. Animals living in very cold climates are usually large with a proportionately small surface area in relation to their body weight (e.g., polar bears and reindeer).
b. An elephant is a very large animal living in a hot climate. To give a greater surface area for heat loss, its skin hangs in folds and it has large, floppy ears.
c. Very small animals with a large surface area in proportion to the body weight usually live in warm climates or hibernate in winter (e.g. harvest mice).
d. Animals such as dogs lose excess heat from their tongues (when panting) and also from the bottom of their feet. It is interesting to note that polar bears have a layer of hair on their feet which helps them to move over frozen surfaces.

ACTIVITIES AND EXPERIMENTS

Types of coverings

1 The children can make picture collections showing suitable clothing for different temperature conditions.

2 The children can make a study of animal coverings, possibly after a visit to a zoo, and decide how well the animals are adapted to their environment.

Absorbers of heat

3 Two bean tins can be used for this study. Paint one with a dull black paint and leave the other shiny. Inside each tin stick a two-pence piece with a blob of candle wax. If both tins are stood at an equal distance from a source of heat (with the two-pence pieces towards the heat), it can be seen that the coin in the black tin falls

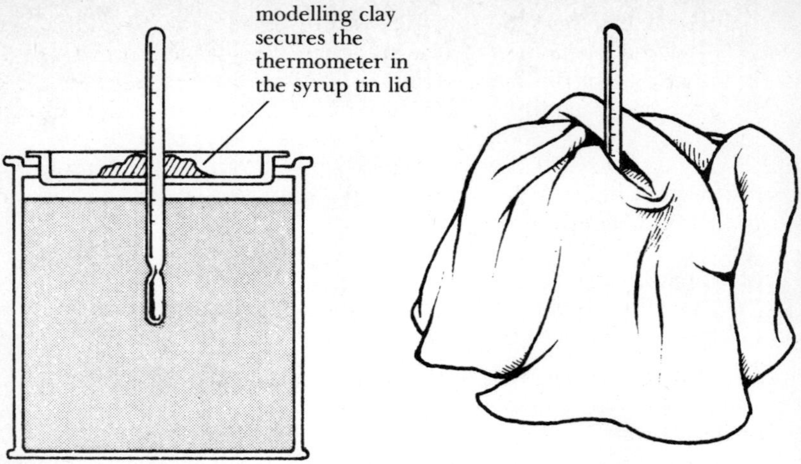

Figure 15 Testing the insulating powers of materials. The syrup tin is filled with hot water and covered with the material to be tested.

first. A radiator or hot water pipe will provide sufficient heat if the tins are placed about 10 cm away. Having tried this the children can experiment with different surfaces — painted white, covered tightly with different coloured papers.

Insulation

4 Older children can be taught to use a thermometer so that more accurate measurements can be made, but many experiments on insulation can be done by comparing the feel of warm surfaces.

a. If tins are filled with hot — not boiling — water and covered with the materials to be tested as illustrated in Figure 15, the temperature can be taken at the start of the experiments, and 30 minutes and 60 minutes later. Tins can be covered with such things as thick woollen material, thin cotton material, felt, paper, fur — in fact, anything that the children can think of. If thermometers are not available, the children can fill the tins (under supervision) with very hot water, and then leave them covered for an hour. Are the surfaces of the tins still too hot to touch?

b. Using a hot-water bottle, filled with hot water, a layer of the material to be tested is placed over it. An ice cube is placed on this and the rate of melting noted. (*Note*: this can be used for comparison only, as the room temperature will also cause the ice to melt, so two or three materials need to be tested at the same time. In this case, all the ice cubes are being subjected to the same room temperature.)

5 It is perfectly possible to cook something in a haybox; children can try this out. A haybox can be made with any large box (although a shiny, tin one would be better — why?). If rolled oats and very hot water are mixed together, then put in a large jar with a lid, they can be put into a haybox cooker, with hay packed all round the jar. The lid is put on the box and it is left overnight. In the morning, the porridge will be both hot and eatable! Can the children think of other ways of keeping food hot?

Problem solving

6 Most of the work on this topic can be done by giving the children problems to solve, and they can then devise their own experiments.

a. If you place your hand flat against a metal surface why does it feel colder than when you put your hand on a polystyrene tile or a piece of wood?

b. Newspaper can be wrapped around things to keep them cold (such as a block of ice-cream) but will it also help to keep things hot?

c. Why does a thick, hairy woollen coat keep you warmer than a thin, smooth one?

d. A string vest is made of cotton, with a lot of spaces in it. How can a garment like this keep you warm?

e. You want to keep your home warm in the winter without wasting too much money on heating it. Think of all the ways in which you can insulate a house against heat loss.

f. Find out about 'survival bags'. Climbers and walkers are advised to carry these with them when they are on excursions. How will these help them to survive exposure to cold conditions? Using a hot-water bottle filled with warm water to represent a person, find out what sort of materials could be used for survival bags.

Experiments with clothes

7 Again children can devise their own experiments. For example, if they make hand coverings of various materials, they can cover their own hands with two different types. Which hand stays the coolest?

The bulbs of thermometers can be wrapped loosely in materials of different colours. These can then be placed near a source of heat or on a warm surface. Which colour absorbs the most heat?

DEVELOPMENTS

1 Ways in which homes are heated and heat conservation.

2 More about heat and the way it moves — convection currents in

air and liquids, radiation across space.
3 Cold-blooded animals and the effects of temperature on these animals.
4 Using heat to help plants grow — the use of cold frames and greenhouses.
5 Soil temperatures and the effects on growth.

LINKS

1 Mathematics — heat and temperature, use of thermometers, comparison of temperatures, Centigrade and Fahrenheit scales.
2 History — how homes have been heated in the past, the story of gas and electricity as heat sources.
3 Geography — temperature and climate, effects on natural vegetation, animal life, produce, clothing.
4 Natural fuels — oil and coal.

RESOURCES AND SUPPORT MATERIAL

Useful apparatus

Thermometers, food tins (with lids removed leaving no sharp edges — using a rotary can opener), electric kettle, hot-water bottles, poylstyrene tiles, old mail order catalogues (pictures of clothing), candle, black and white matt and gloss paint.

General reference books

General Science Book, 2 C. Windridge (Schofield and Sims).
Look! Primary Science Teachers' Guide, A C. Gilbert and P. Matthews (Addison-Wesley).
Investigations, Part 2 Science 5/13 (Macdonald Educational).

Children's books

Introducing Science, 6: Heat S. Jackson (Blackie).
The Zoo Book G. Standring (Macdonald Educational).
Coal B. Gunston (Franklin Watts).
Animals in Winter V. Luff (A. & C. Black).

Other resources

1 *A Centenary of Service* (A history of electricity in the home) — The Electricity Council, 30 Millbank, London, SW1P 4RD.
2 Soil thermometer — Philip Harris Ltd (address see Section 21).
3 Very large wall thermometer — ESA Creative Learning Ltd (address see Section 21).
4 *The Walrus and the Polar Bear* (adaptations for life in the Arctic)

(filmstrip and cassette) — The Slide Centre (address see Section 21).
5 *Animals of the World* (series of seven filmstrips or slide sets) — The Slide Centre (address see Section 21).

2 Air is there

Air is all around us, and children are well aware of this. They will glibly tell you that you have got to breathe air or you would die, but they seem to be unsure as to whether it is really 'something'. Older children will understand that an empty bottle is not actually empty but that it contains air, although they cannot see it and they do not know how they can demonstrate that it is there. Once children can see for themselves that air exists and occupies space, they will find it much easier to appreciate the properties of air and the uses to which it can be put.

GENERAL NOTES

1 Air has definite properties.

a. It is a gas made up of a mixture of other gases — about 78 percent is nitrogen, 21 percent oxygen and the rest consists of small quantities of other gases such as carbon dioxide.
b. It is invisible.
c. It can be felt and contained, and it occupies space.

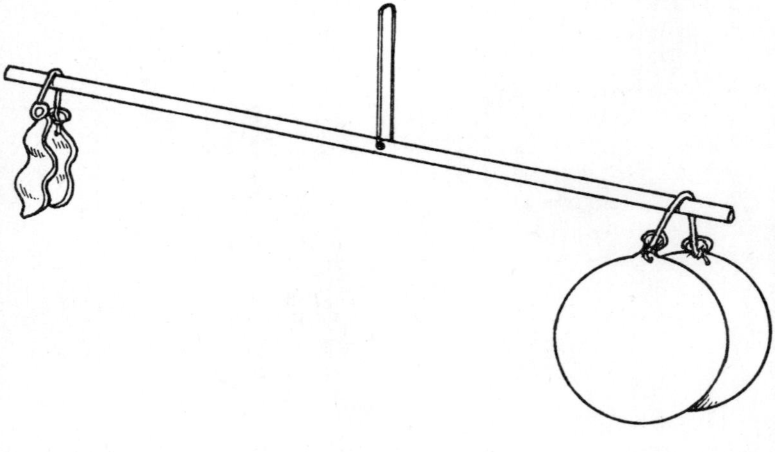

Figure 16 Showing that air has weight. The rod must be carefully balanced before the balloons at one end are inflated.

d. It is less dense than water so air bubbles will rise to the surface of water.
e. It exerts pressure, pushing in all directions.

2 A space from which all air has been extracted is called a vacuum.
3 Oxygen is essential for life — all living things need oxygen — and fuels will not burn without it.
4 Childen can see that air exists by observing some of the ways in which air can be used. For example

a. Air currents — kite flying, bird flight, aircraft.
b. Wind (moving air) — windmills, sailing ships, seed dispersal, musical instruments through which air is blown.
c. Filling with air — balloons, car tyres, bicycle tyres.
d. Using air resistance — parachute.
e. Using air pressure — syringe, bird drinker.

ACTIVITIES AND EXPERIMENTS

Air as a substance
1 The following experiments are designed to demonstrate the existence of air.

a. Squash a plastic bottle quickly and feel the air come out.
b. Get a plastic bottle with a screw-on lid. Screw it up tightly and try to squash the bottle. The air inside prevents the sides being pushed in.
c. Hold the neck of a plastic bottle under water and squeeze the bottle. The air can be seen bubbling out.
d. Blow up a balloon or a flat bicycle tyre.

Air has weight
2 Use a wooden ruler or piece of dowel about 1 m long. Drill a small hole in the centre to take a thread and hang up the dowel by the thread. Get it to balance exactly by adding tiny pieces of plasticine to the lighter end. Now hang two or three empty balloons on each end — using a thread tied loosely round each neck. Again check that the dowel is balanced. Very carefully remove the balloons from one end and blow them up (i.e. filling them with air). Hang them back on the dowel by the same threads and in the same place. The balloons containing the air will weigh more than the others and will tilt the dowel (see Figure 16).

Air takes up room
3 Once the children have tried these simple experiments they will be able to think out some more for themselves.

a. If a funnel with a narrow stem is put into a bottle and the space round it is sealed with plasticine, the children can see what happens when they try to pour water into the bottle. The water will either stay in the funnel — because there is no room in the bottle — or will go in spurts, with the air bubbling out — there is only room for the water if some of the air can escape.

If the plasticine is taken away the water can run freely. Why?

b. If a jar is inverted and pushed into water (a small aquarium is useful for these experiments) the water will rise so far, but will not fill the jar. The air can be compressed, but it still occupies space and the water cannot get in. If a dry tissue is put in the bottom of the jar before it is inverted, the children can see that the jar can be pushed right under the water, but the tissue remains dry. Does it make any difference how deep the water is? What happens if the jar is tilted?

Air exerts pressure

4 Children like the well-known experiment of sliding a card over the surface of a jar or tumbler completely full of water, and then inverting it. This needs to be done smoothly (a jerk will dislodge the card). Air pressure holds the card on and the water does not spill.

5 Suckers stay on a wall because air is squeezed out as they are pushed on to the wall; the air pushing on the outside holds the sucker firmly fixed. If a sucker with a hole in it is used the experiment will not work.

6 A simple syringe is used to draw water into the barrel. As the plunger is pulled upwards the air pressure inside is reduced and water flows into the barrel because the outside air pushes down on the surface of the water. Can the children suck water into a plastic bottle in the same way?

7 If the children keep small mammals or budgerigars, a simple drinker can be made for them. The children need to experiment first so that they realize that pressure will keep a column of water in a bottle. If the bottle is completely filled with water and then inverted into a bowl of water, the water in the bottle will remain there. As soon as the neck of the bottle is lifted out of the bowl of water, it empties. This fact can be used to make the drinker (see Figure 17). The air pressure keeps the water in the bottle. As the animal drinks, the neck of the bottle comes above the water level and water spills out until the neck is covered again.

Air resistance

8 Get the children to run across the playground holding a piece of strong cardboard or hardboard (about 1 m^2) in front, like a shield and then to try again holding the board out horizontally so that its front edge 'cuts into' the air. Does the position of the board make any difference?

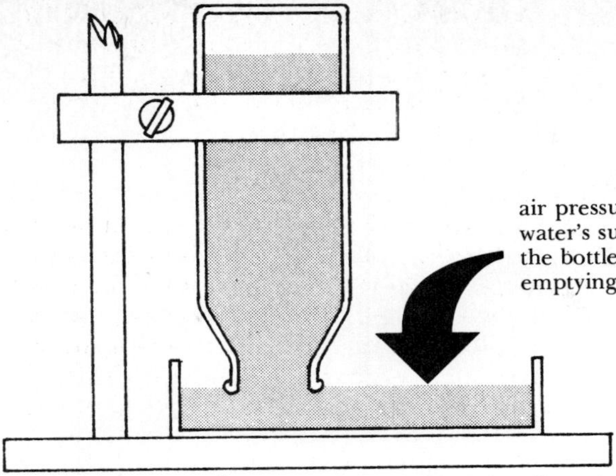

Figure 17 A drinker for birds or small animals.

9 Get two pieces of paper (about 30 cm × 30 cm). Try dropping these from a height (standing on a table). Drop them flat and edgewise; crumple one into a ball before dropping it. Why does the sheet dropped flat glide to the ground while the crumpled sheet falls straight?
10 Make flying toys — darts and paper aeroplanes. Which fly the best? Have a competition to see who can make the best paper flyer, the winner being the one that stays up the longest.
11 Make parachutes with squares of material with threads tied to each corner and then attach these threads to some sort of weight — its size will depend on the size of the parachute. Having made this very simple version and tried it out, the children can design their own models, and they will probably want to find out what happens if the parachute has a hole cut in it, after seeing films of parachute jumps on the television. What makes a good parachute? Does size make any difference to performance? What difference does shape make?

Moving air
12 Ask the children to think of all the indications they can of moving air. Examples include

a. Wind moving leaves and branches, with leaves being blown along the road.
b. Washing flapping on the line.
c. Feeling the wind on one's face.
d. Wind filling sails of sailing boats and moving them.
e. Birds gliding on air currents.
f. Using a fan.

DEVELOPMENTS

1 Air as a supporter of burning and respiration.
2 Respiration of different living things.
3 The flight of birds and the structure of feathers.
4 Air pressure and barometers.

LINKS

1 Craft — model making (e.g., simple sailing boats, jet-propelled toys using balloons as the propelling agent, model aeroplanes and gliders).
2 History — the story of flight.
3 Geography — wind forces (Beaufort Scale).
4 Music — instruments depending on blown air.

RESOURCES AND SUPPORT MATERIAL

Useful apparatus

Plastic bottles, glass bottles and jars, plastic funnels, plasticine, thin string, strong cardboard sheets, balloons, lengths of dowel, small aquaria, and plastic bowls, thin wire, pieces of wood, small saws, cartridge paper, pieces of fabric of different sizes and types.

General reference books

What is Air: Science Horizons Level, 2a P. Hine (Macmillan Education).
Look! Primary Science Teachers' Guide, A C. Gilbert and P. Matthews (Addison-Wesley).
Science and Air S.F. King (Hart-Davis).

Children's books

Air D. Lloyd (Methuen).
Air is All Around You F. M. Bramley (A. & C. Black).
Air, Wind and Flight F. Newing and R. Bowood (Ladybird Books).
Air Travel (New Reference Library) (Macdonald Educational).
In the Air D. Kincaid and P.S. Coles (Hulton Educational).
Amazing Air H. Smith (Methuen).

Other resources

1 *Air, Wind and Flight* (filmstrip) — The Slide Centre (address see Section 21).
2 *The Hovercraft* (filmstrip) — The Slide Centre (address see Section 21).
3 *Man Must Fly: The History of Flight* and *How an Aircraft Flies* (two

filmstrips with cassettes) — VP Educational Resources (address see Section 21).

4 Wind vane, wind meter and wind speed indicator — Philip Harris Ltd (address see Section 21).

13 Metals all around

It is relatively simple to classify something as being made of metal, but it is not always easy to decide exactly which metal has been used. Although children like identifying and naming things, it is more important that first they become familiar with the general properties of metals. After this they can find out more about specific metals and how they are used. At this stage they can also be introduced to some of the metals seen less frequently.

GENERAL NOTES

1 Metals have been known and used for over 5000 years. With the onset of the Industrial Revolution they began to play a much more important role in the lives of everyone.
2 The metals most likely to be known by children are hard, strong, shiny, malleable (i.e. they can be beaten into flat sheets), ductile (i.e. they can be pulled into wire) and have a high melting point (e.g., iron, copper, silver, gold). The metals most likely to be met by children include iron (and steel), copper, aluminium, tin, lead, brass, silver, gold, platinum, zinc, mercury and pewter. In contrast, lead is a relatively soft, dull metal with a low melting point and mercury is liquid.
3 Many metals are good conductors of electricity (e.g., silver, copper, mercury) and of heat.
4 Some metals are alloys — they are made of two or more metals combined or are a combination of a metal and a non-metallic element. Table 3 shows examples of alloys and their special properties.

Table 3

Alloy	Constituents	Properties
Steel	Iron and carbon	Stronger and harder than iron alone.
Solder	Lead and tin	Low melting point.
Brass	Copper and zinc	Malleable and easily shaped
Stainless steel	Iron, chromium and nickel	Resists rust.

5 Iron is one of the commonest metals found and is one of the most important. It is easily extracted from its ores and can be made into the major construction material, steel. It can be magnetized and its history is extremely interesting. (*Note*: Anything that can be strongly magnetized contains one or more of the metals iron, cobalt and nickel.)

6 Copper can be pulled into very fine wires (i.e. it is ductile). Because of its very high electrical conductivity, its most important use is for electric wiring. Mixed with tin it makes the alloy bronze, which was first used about 3000 years ago to make tools, weapons, ornamental figures, bowls and jewellery.

7 The precious metals include gold, silver and platinum. Gold is the most malleable and ductile of all the metals and can be beaten into very fine sheets (gold leaf) which can be used for decoration. Pure gold is too soft for general use and so is alloyed with other metals (e.g., copper). The purity of gold is measured in carats (a carat is 1/24th part) so an 18-carat gold ring is 18/24ths or 75 percent pure gold. There are several metals closely related to platinum including palladium, iridium and rhodium.

8 Rusting (i.e. oxidation) of iron is a very important economic feature, and the prevention of rusting is a major concern. It is easy to see how quickly a car body begins to rust, and most iron structures have patches of rust showing. For rusting, oxygen and water are necessary, so prevention is concerned with covering the surface of the iron so that these cannot reach it. Several different methods of protection are used.

a. Food 'tins' are not really made of tin but of iron covered with a thin layer of tin to prevent water and oxygen reaching the iron.
b. Oil and paint act as rust retarders.
c. Stainless steel contains chromium which does not rust.

9 There are many other metals that are not used in any quantity either because they are scarce, are difficult to work or do not have properties for which there is an immediate need. Titanium is a metal not used until recent years but it is now being increasingly used in the aircraft industry because it can withstand corrosion and is extremely strong and light.

ACTIVITIES AND EXPERIMENTS

Collections of metals

1 Make a collection of metal objects and try to decide why metal was used to make them. Why is metal used for saucepans? Could they be made of anything else? Why is metal the best material? Why are knives, scissors, needles and woodworking tools made of metal?

Could any type of metal be used? Why is hardened steel best for those with cutting edges? Try and include some uncommon or not easily noticed objects — electric light bulb with its tungsten filament, zip fastener, wire closures for plastic bags, umbrella spokes.
2 Make and display a collection of decorative metal objects. This could include such things as jewellery (base metals as well as precious metals), a pewter tankard, objects with inlaid metal, a book with gold leaf on the cover and so on.
3 Make a table like Table 4 of the uses for some of the commoner metals

Table 4

Metal	Uses
Aluminium	Kettles, saucepans, cooking foil
Tin	Coating food containers, alloyed with lead to make solder
Silver	Cutlery, jewellery, also one of the best conductors of electricity

Uses of metals
4 List every metal object that can be seen in one room. This will give some idea of the extensive use of metals, and can be made into a competition (who noticed the nails in the floor boards, the key, staples holding a book together or sandal buckles?).
5 If some samples of metals can be obtained they can be tested for hardness by scratching with a sharp nail. Which is the hardest, lead or copper? Which metals appear hard enough to be used for making tools?
6 Various tools can be tried on pieces of metal. Can it be filed, drilled (using a hand drill) or hammered? (Does the hammering dent or scratch the surface?)
7 Make a collection of wire and wire objects. Why is wire so useful? Name some of the uses of wire (electric wires, bag closures, bundling flowers, coat hangers, fences). Test the wires for strength by repeatedly bending them, by cutting with wire cutters and hitting with a hammer. Is the wire being tested suitable for its specific use? Where is soft wire useful? Where is it best to use hard wire? Find out about cables made from numerous wire strands.

Rusting
8 Using nails find out how long it takes for them to start rusting. Will they rust if they are kept absolutely dry or if they are kept under water? Using large nails test ways of preventing rust — painting, oiling, covering with grease, wrapping in cloth, wrapping in paper

or any other suggestions made by the children. Put the nails somewhere damp and see which start to rust and how long it takes. The children can find out if other metals are affected by water and air. Is the oxidization of other metals a factor affecting their use?

Magnetism

9 Although nickel and cobalt can be magnetized, the children are not very likely to have these metals available and so magnetism can be used to identify iron and objects containing iron. If they are given a collection of various small metal objects, they can sort out those made of iron, and can find out if steel can be magnetized. Children are very inclined to think that any common metals can be picked up with a magnet and are often surprised when they find that there are many things that will not respond.

Using a mercury thermometer

10 If children are shown mercury, this must be done by the teacher; the children should not be allowed to touch it. They can best see one of its uses by working with large laboratory thermometers, when they can see how its expansion can be used as an indicator of temperature. This is also an opportunity to teach them how to use a thermometer accurately and sensibly.

DEVELOPMENTS

1 Expansion and contraction of metals.
2 Springs.
3 Finding out more about other metals and seeing examples of some of these.
4 More about the extraction of metals from their ores.

LINKS

1 History — the Iron Age and the Bronze Age, the story of the car, the story of the wheel.
2 Geography — the Gold Rush. Where are metals found? Countries of origin.
3 Craft — using metals to make things (e.g., jewellery, small dishes), using metal tools for woodwork.
4 Art — the story of iron and steel (told in pictures), looking at photographs of particular metal artifacts (e.g., the mask of Tutankhamun, Viking finds at Sutton Hoo), wrought iron work, the work of the blacksmith (if possible, see work being done in a smithy).

RESOURCES AND SUPPORT MATERIAL

Useful apparatus

Files, hammers, nails, oil, grease, thermometers, needles, knives (dining room-type), scissors, wire of all kinds, pliers, wire cutters, hand drill, strong magnets.

General reference books

Metals: Background Information Science 5/13 (Macdonald Educational).
Metals: Stages 1 and 2 Science 5/13 (Macdonald Educational).
Junior Science Source Book J. W. Bainbridge *et al.* (Collins).
Rainbow Fact Book of Science M. W. Dempsey (W. H. Smith).
General Science, 2 C. Windridge (Schofield and Sims).

Children's books

Metals R. Kerrod (Macdonald Educational).
Coins; Metals; The Motor Car (Junior Reference Library) (Macdonald Educational).

Other resources

1 *Minerals and their Sources* (filmstrip) — Hugh Baddeley Productions (address see Section 21).
2 Pamphlets and information — Unilever Educational Productions (address see Section 21), Stainless Steel Development Association, 65 Vincent Square, London S.W.1.
3 *Metals* (16 mm film for purchase only) — Educational Foundation for Visual Aids (EFVA), Paxton Place, Gipsy Road, London SE27 9SR.
4 *Craft of the Early Metalworker* (filmstrip) — EFVA.
5 *The Blacksmith* (16 mm film for hire) — Petroleum Film Bureau, 4 Brook Street, Hanover Square, London W.1.

14 Water on tap

Water covers about 70 percent of the Earth's surface. Most of it is contained in the oceans and some of it is in a permanently frozen state in the form of glaciers and ice sheets.

Water is essential for all living plants and animals; a reliable water supply was one of the first requisites of settlement. Historically, villages grew up where there was a pond or where the underground supply could be made available using wells or springs. In many parts of the world, this still applies, with the drying up of the water supply threatening the lives of people and animals.

In this country, it is still possible to find pumps, troughs, wells and village ponds. Although some spring water is suitable for drinking (and is still used), water for houses is usually stored in reservoirs and is then purified to remove rubbish and harmful bacteria.

GENERAL NOTES

1 Water, which is the most important compound found on Earth, is made up of hydrogen and oxygen; it can be a liquid, a vapour (steam) or a solid (ice). Water (H_2O) constantly evaporates from the oceans. When the humidity of the air reaches saturation point (i.e. when air contains the maximum amount of water vapour that it can hold at a particular temperature) droplets of water form. These droplets mass together forming clouds and it is from these clouds that rain falls.

2 Water that falls on land runs into streams (and subsequently into rivers and lakes) or it soaks into the ground where a great deal of it is taken up by plants.

3 Water, as it seeps through the ground, dissolves minerals in the rock. Some of these mineral salts (e.g., calcium salts) make it difficult for soap to form a lather; this is termed 'hard' water. Some salts, such as fluorides, are beneficial; fluorides prevent tooth decay.

4 Water for household use is filtered and chlorinated as shown in Figure 18 — filtering removes solids including some of the bacteria and the very small amount of chlorine added kills any harmful bacteria. Filter beds are built up of layers of sand and gravel that trap mud, bacteria and any rubbish. Water from reservoirs is trickled over them.

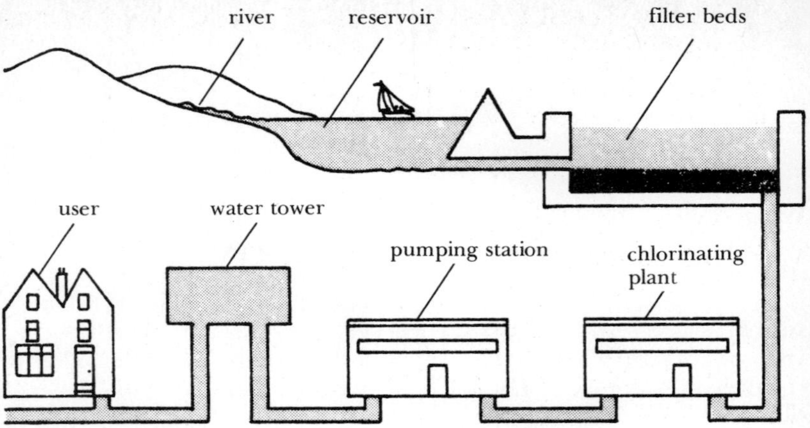

Figure 18 Water's journey from the reservoir to the user.

5 Water in the home is used for drinking, cooking, washing, cleaning and flushing the lavatory.
6 Water normally boils at about 100°C or 212°F (salts dissolved in the water increase the temperature at which it boils). Although pure water boils at 100°C at sea-level, changes in pressure can alter the boiling point. When water boils, it changes into water vapour.
7 Water freezes at 0°C or 32°F and changes into ice. Ice takes up more room than the water from which it has formed and this can be shown by filling a bottle to the top and then putting it in the freezer (without a lid on). The frozen water forms a peak of ice sticking out at the top (this happens to milk on very cold days when bottle tops can be seen sitting on columns of frozen milk protruding from the bottles). Water freezing can cause burst water pipes. These bursts are often not apparent until the weather gets warmer when the water thaws and can escape from the broken pipes.
8 Water evaporates all the time, but the rate of evaporation is increased when the water is heated (i.e. when the weather is warm). When there is a great deal of water vapour in the air, it is said to be humid. Hot, humid conditions are particularly uncomfortable because sweat on the skin cannot evaporate readily and therefore does not have a cooling effect.

ACTIVITIES AND EXPERIMENTS

Uses of water

1 Make a list of all the ways in which water is used in your home and estimate how much water *you* use in one day.

2 Make a survey of the water supply of a house or school. The following questions may serve as a starter.

a. Which rooms have a water supply?
b. Where is the cold water stored?
c. Where is the hot water stored, and how is it heated?
d. How many taps are there in the building?
e. How many lavatories are there in the building?
f. Where does the water for this building originate?
g. Is it hard or soft water? (See Experiment 8).

Evaporation
3 Put the same amount of water in several saucers and note how long it takes the water to evaporate from each of them. Leave them in different places.

a. Near an open window, in a draught.
b. Outside (if it is not raining!).
c. In a warm place (i.e. near a radiator or in the sun).
d. In a refrigerator.
e. In a cupboard.
f. Other places suggested by the children.

Under what sort of conditions does water evaporate quickly? Can the children devise an experiment to show whether or not the weather conditions affect the speed of evaporation? (Will water evaporate more quickly on a warm, dry day or on a warm, humid day?) Having tried out some of these experiments, the children should be able to see what happens to puddles after the rain and how they gradually disappear.

Condensation
4 If one breathes on a cold surface, the water vapour in the exhaled air will condense and form small droplets. Why does water vapour condense on the windows on some days and not on others?
5 Using steam from hot water — the water need not be boiling but it needs to be very hot so it must be used under supervision — find ways of making it condense. Will it condense on warm as well as cold surfaces? Will it condense on any surface? Use a hair drier to simulate the demister of a car.

Filtering
6 Mix a handful of soil with a litre of water, and then try various ways of filtering it to clear out the mud. Try filtering it through cloth or a paper towel. Line a funnel with cotton wool and filter through this. Make a model filter bed using a large plant pot (see Figure 19). Try other materials in the filter bed.

Figure 19 A filter made from a plant pot.

Water content of food

7 Most of the foods we eat contain water. Weigh a slice of bread then either leave it in the sun or put it in a warm oven until it is hard and dry. What does it weigh now? How much water did it contain? Weigh an apple before cutting it into slices and drying it in the oven. How much water did it contain? What proportion of an apple is water?

Hardness of water

8 Use a bottle that will hold about 500 ml and that has a secure cork or stopper. Mark the bottle about one-third of the way up and fill up to this point with the water to be tested. Add one pinch of soap powder — it must be soap and not detergent — and shake. Does it form a lather that will last for a minute? Go on adding the powder, one pinch at a time, until a lasting lather is formed. Try different types of water (e.g., rain, pond, tap water from different areas, sea water and boiled water) but always use the same amount of cold water. Draw up a chart to show the hardest and the softest waters, and try to answer some questions.

a. Why is rain water soft?
b. Does boiling soften water?
c. Does the soap lather best with hot or cold water?
d. Would it be easy to wash in sea water?

Freezing
9 Put water in various containers, filling to the top and freeze in a refrigerator. What happens to the water as it freezes? Fill a small, screw-topped plastic bottle. Seal it firmly and freeze it. What happens? (The bottle will either crack or be pushed out at the sides, depending on the strength of the bottle.)

Cleaning
10 Water is used for a great deal of the cleaning in a home; this can be used as a basis for further work. Washing powders can be tested to see which is best for a particular area and which is the most economical. Dissolve a teaspoonful of the powder to be tested in a jar of warm water. Put in a square of dirty material — old sheeting, which has been put on the classroom floor and walked on all morning and then torn into 10 cm squares — and stir for exactly one minute. Test each powder the same way and compare results.

DEVELOPMENTS

1 Siphons and how they work.
2 Making soap.
3 Water as a solvent.
4 The rain cycle.
5 Distillation.

LINKS

1 See also **Living in water** (Section 1).
2 Mathematics — comparative cost of washing powders and washing-up liquids.
3 Home economics — cost of using water in the home (i.e. water rates with extra costs for using hosepipes), cooking and water temperatures, pressure cookery, making drinks.
4 Geography — sources of water, position of reservoirs, water in deserts.
5 History — how village life grew up around the village pond, the story of water supplies, the importance of drainage and sanitation as towns grew bigger.
6 Environmental studies — water pollution and conservation.

RESOURCES AND SUPPORT MATERIAL

Useful apparatus
Saucers or flat dishes, plastic bottles, glass jars or beakers, electric kettle, old sheeting, blotting paper, filter paper, plastic funnels, large clay flower pot, cotton wool, plastic teaspoons, samples of soaps and detergents, packet of soap powder or soap flakes.

General reference books
Water W. Gunston (Macdonald Educational).
Exploring Things (Science Happenings Book 4) M. Holt (Ginn).
Look! Primary Science Teachers' Book, A C. Gilbert and P. Matthews (Addison-Wesley).

Children's books
Houses and Homes (Science and a Topic) D. Kincaid and P. S. Coles (Hulton).
Science Workshop, 2 I. Finch (BBC/Longman).

Other resources
1 Resource sheet on clean water — Centre for World Development Education, 128 Buckingham Palace Road, London SW1 9SH.
2 *Water* (slide set from Looking Around series) — The Slide Centre (address see Section 21).
3 *Water* (filmstrip) — The Slide Centre.
4 *How We Get Pure Water* (filmstrip and cassette commentary) — The Slide Centre.
5 Visit to a reservoir and a pumping station.

15 Sticking it together

An adhesive is a substance that sticks or adheres to something else. Most children will be more inclined to use the words glue or gum, but strictly speaking glue means those adhesives that are of animal or vegetable origin. Having said this, it hardly matters and children will happily 'glue' something together when they are actually using a synthetic adhesive. Younger children tend to say that they are going to 'stick' something and often assume that any sticky substance can be used for this purpose; this, in itself, is worth investigating.

The chemistry of adhesives is far too advanced for primary children, but they can learn a lot about organizing a piece of simple research by deciding upon ways of testing the usefulness and efficiency of adhesives, and by trying out some old-fashioned recipes. They may even find that some very cheap, easily obtained materials are better for some jobs than bought adhesives!

GENERAL NOTES

1 The cohesion of an adhesive depends largely on the way in which it changes from a liquid (or semi-liquid) to a solid form. Sometimes adhesives are liquefied by heating and they return to their solid form on cooling. More commonly, an adhesive is dissolved in some sort of solvent; this solvent evaporates into the air leaving the solid adhesive. Sometimes the solvent is water — postage stamps have an adhesive that can be softened by wetting the stamp. As the water evaporates, the stamp remains stuck to the envelope.

2 Sometimes two separate liquids are mixed together and these react chemically to form a strong solid.

3 One glue is made by heating animal bones in steam under pressure; the bones are reduced to a sticky liquid which then sets solid. This is an adhesive that is heated in a little water to soften it and has been used for hundreds of years in furniture making.

4 Children will have heard of the 'super' glues. These can be bought quite easily, but should only be used under very strict supervision. Having been told that these adhesives will stick fingers together or lips closed so that it is impossible to open them, they may be tempted to find out if this is true. (It is!)

5 Glues and other adhesives have hundreds of uses. For example

a. Labelling — sticking labels on to boxes, jars and other goods,

making boxes and cartons, sealing envelopes.
b. Packaging.
c. Sealing — windows, car components.
d. Household — fixing work surfaces, furniture, wallpaper, ceramic tiles, flooring.
e. Clothing — parts of shoes, rubber boots, some leather garments.
f. Mending — glass, china, wooden items.
g. Hobbies — model making.

6 There are numerous adhesives on the market, some classed as general-purpose glues and some intended for specific use. Some types of adhesives with examples of trade names that the children may meet include

a. Epoxy resins — Araldite (used by mixing two liquids together).
b. PVA resin emulsions — Marvin Medium.
c. Latex adhesives — Copydex.
d. Various pastes used for sticking paper — Cow Gum (used for such jobs as mounting photographs), Polycell (wallpaper adhesives).
e. Impact adhesives — Evo-Stick.
f. Adhesives for ceramic tiles — Polyfix.
g. Adhesive tapes and labels. — Sellotape.

There are, however, many more and it is not difficult to collect samples.

Note: Some adhesives contain toluene di-isocyanate (TDI) and these are the ones associated with glue sniffing. None of these should be used in schools. If in any doubt about a particular sample, do not use it until you are sure about what it contains. If necessary consult the manufacturer, but reputable firms supplying schools do not include these in their catalogues or they give very clear indications of the contents of their adhesives.

ACTIVITIES AND EXPERIMENTS

Collections of adhesives

1 Make as large a collection as possible of adhesives. Read the instructions and note the manufacturers' claims and recommendations. Will each adhesive do what it says provided that the instructions are carried out properly? Note if the glue is inflammable. Some claim to stick 'anything to anything'. Are there any adhesives that will do this?

2 Make a chart similar to the one that follows and test several of the adhesives in the collection. Try as many experiments as possible. These could be done in groups (i.e. paper — sticking to paper, card, glass, metal, wood, plastic, ceramic, leather, cloth, stone, etc.).

	Will it stick . . .?					
	glass to glass	wood to wood	metal to wood	paper to wood	card to glass	plastic to plastic
Glue A						
Glue B						
Glue C						
Glue D						

Strengths of adhesives

3 Test the strength of adhesive hooks (the type used for hanging up small kitchen items).

4 Test the strength of different glues. In order to make a proper comparison each glue must be used on the same type of material, allowed to dry and must be subjected to the same tests. Use strips of wood, each about 12 cm × 4 cm. Drill a hole in one end of each strip and tie a string loop through each hole (using strong string). Stick two strips together overlapping 2 cm. Hang the strips up by one loop and hang a tin on the other loop (see Figure 20). Add weights to the tin and see what weight is needed to separate the strips. Devise other ways of testing the strength of adhesives. Were the adhesives used intended for wood? Try the experiment above but with the ends of the wood butted together instead of overlapping.

5 The children may think of interesting ways to test adhesive tapes but they could make parcels by wrapping boxes in stout paper and then sealing the paper with adhesive tape. Will the tape remain secure if the parcels are knocked about? What happens if the parcel is left out in the rain?

6 Test wallpaper adhesives and ready-pasted wallpaper.

Alternatives to proprietary adhesives

7 Try substances other than proprietary adhesives and see if they will stick things together. For example, try jam, treacle, resin from trees (spruce, fir or the outside of horse chestnut buds), paint, nail varish or anything else that the children can suggest.

8 Collect old-fashioned recipes or ideas for home-made glues. Try making these and using them, and decide how effective they are. Here are some examples.

a. Flour and water paste — mix a tablespoonful of flour with a little cold water to make a smooth, creamy liquid. Add boiling water, stirring until the paste thickens. What can this be used for? Are there any disadvantages? Many people used to use this for hanging wallpaper but they often added a spoonful of disinfectant to it. Why?

b. My grandmother, if she had to replace a tile round a fireplace or on a wall, always painted both the tile and the wall with a fairly thick layer of condensed milk. The tile was pressed firmly into place and left to dry without touching for about a week. Find out if this idea worked.

c. Break up egg white with a fork. This can be used as a glue to stick china. Coat each broken edge with egg white and leave to dry. Coat the edges again and stick together. Hold the broken pieces together in some way and leave to dry for about 24 hours. This was found in an old recipe book. Does it work?

Finding the right adhesive for the job

9 Decide on various jobs to be done and find the best adhesive for this.

a. Sticking down vinyl floor covering.
b. Making a cardboard model.
c. Sticking the edges of a carpet.
d. Mending a glass vase.
e. Sticking polystyrene tiles on a ceiling.

DEVELOPMENTS

1 Natural adhesives — spider's web, attachment of limpets to rocks, sticky secretion of insectiverous plants such as sundew.
2 Other old recipes — making candles, furniture polish, soap.

LINKS

1 Craft — model making and collage using adhesives.
2 History — the use of adhesives in furniture making.

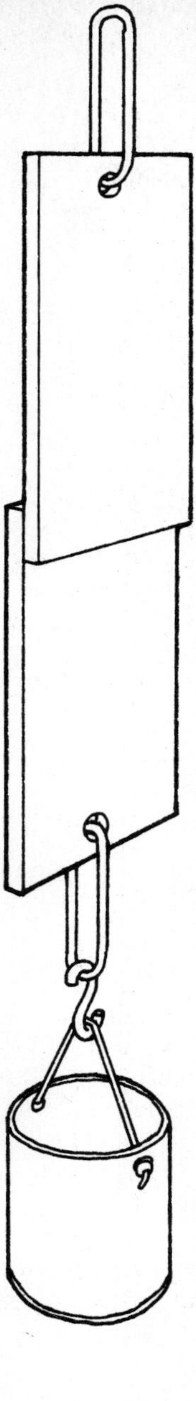

Figure 20 Testing the adhesive power of a glue.

RESOURCES AND SUPPORT MATERIAL

Useful apparatus

Collection of adhesives of all kinds, wooden lath, small hacksaw, wood drill, strong string, bean cans (lids removed with a rotary can opener), weights, paper and card, wood off-cuts, metal pieces, plastic pieces, bits of fabric and leather, trays or plastic sheet to work on, brushes, tiles.

General reference books

Science and Technology M. Bisacre *et al.* (ed.) (Marshall Cavendish).
Junior Science Source Book J. W. Bainbridge *et al.* (Collins).

Children's books

Model Ideas H. Pluckrose (ed.) (Evans Brothers).
Wooden Toys (Handcraft Series) (EP Publishing).
Kites (Handcraft Series) (EP Publishing)
Know How Book of Action Toys H. Amery (Usborne Publishing).

Other resources

1 Adhesives — Nottingham Educational Supplies, 17 Ludlow Hill Road, West Bridgford, Nottingham NG2 6HD; Dryad, PO Box 38, Northgates, Leicester LE1 9BU.
2 Information — Copydex Ltd, 1 Torquay Street, London W2.
3 *Art and Craft Education* (monthly magazine) — Scholastic Publications.
4 Model-making materials — Solarbo Ltd, Commerce Way, Lancing, Sussex BN15 8TE.

16 Yarns, fibres and fabrics

Wool, cotton and linen yarns are made of very fine fibres, twisted together to make yarns. These yarns can be made into fabrics — either looped together (knitted) or woven. Children often have the opportunity to work with yarns and fabrics in craft lessons, but rarely look at them to see how they are made or used.

They may know that many of these yarns come from natural sources and that there are a large number of man-made yarns, each with its own particular properties. It is to give children the chance to find out more about these materials that the suggestions below have been made. There is so much work that they could do that this can only be a brief outline, but teachers can develop their own ideas and can link this topic with many other subjects.

GENERAL NOTES

1 Fibres are single threads — a human hair is a good example — and these can best be looked at by obtaining some sheep fleece. The pieces found on hedges or fences will be sufficient. Some fibres are man-made (e.g., nylon, rayon) but, like the other fibres, have to be twisted together to make yarns.

2 Natural fibres are from plant or animal sources.

a. Cotton is the most important vegetable fibre. It is produced from the seed pod of the cotton plant. Each fibre is about 30–65 mm long.

b. Flax is the fibre used to make linen. The fibres come from the stem of the plant. Each flax fibre is 400–600 mm long and is very strong. Fabrics made from flax stand a great deal of wear (e.g., tablecloths, handkerchiefs, sheets).

c. Other vegetable fibres include jute, used for making sacks and bags, and for backing rugs and carpets, hemp, made into sacking and canvas, and sisal, used for making cords, ropes and mats but not fabrics.

d. The term wool is usually used to denote the fibres from sheep, although fibres from other animals are often called wool (e.g., angora wool from a rabbit, cashmere wool from a type of goat). The woollen industry began in Britain; by 55 BC wool was being spun and woven into yarn. The other main animal fibres that can be made into yarns include camel, alpaca and goat but all types of animal hair and fur can be used.

e. Silk is an animal fibre, that comes from the cocoon of the silk moth. When the caterpillars pupate, they spin a covering of fine, strong fibres in long, continuous threads. The history of the production of silk is a very fascinating one, beginning in China in about 2600 BC.

3 The best known man-made fibres are the polyamides (e.g. nylon), the polyesters (e.g. Terylene, Dacron) and the acrylics (e.g., Acrilan, Courtelle, Orlan), but there are many others and it is very difficult to identify them.

4 Fabric manufacture involves the making of yarn which is then made into material.

a. The first stage is spinning. The fine fibres have to be twisted together to make a continuous yarn which is both thicker and stronger than the fibres on their own. Two or more lengths of yarn can be used together (i.e. plied) to make an even stronger and more stable thread. Spinning can be done using a very primitive spindle, a spinning wheel, or the complicated machinery used in the textile factories.

b. To make fabrics the yarns have to be linked together in some way. Knitted fabrics have the yarns looped together, while woven fabrics are made by passing one group of yarns (the weft) over and under another group (the warp). Weaving can be done on the simplest looms or even between the branches of trees, but the vast quantities of fabrics used in the world today are produced in modern factories. To find out more about yarn and fabric manufacture read one of the books suggested in the bibliography at the end of the section.

5 The natural colours of fibres are limited, but yarns can be dyed before being made into fabrics. Some fabrics are printed after having been woven.

ACTIVITIES AND EXPERIMENTS

Collection of yarns

1 Collect as many samples as possible of different yarns. Unpick these to get the individual fibres. These can be looked at with a good lens or under a microscope. How do cotton and wool fibres differ?

2 Investigate different yarns by finding the following facts.

a. Origin (if known) — wool, cotton, nylon, mixture of wool and nylon, etc.

b. Strength.
c. Elasticity — how much does the yarn stretch? Does it return to its original length after being stretched?
d. Observation — unpick the yarn. Is it plied? Are there many fibres in each thread? Look at the yarn and the fibres under a good lens or microscope. Does it look like a natural fibre? Is it made of one type of fibre or more? Is it dyed?
e. What is it used for — knitting wool, thread taken from a blanket, dress material, etc.

3 Test the strength of yarns by fixing lengths of yarn to a clamp and then hanging weights in a net attached to the other end. What is the breaking point of each yarn used? Which yarns stretch before breaking? How much do they stretch? Could you find the strength of individual fibres? (Start with a hair).

Classification by burning

4 Pieces of yarn or fabric can be held with long tongs and burnt in a candle flame. The candle should be placed on a metal tray or large tin lid and, obviously, the whole experiment should be well supervised. The questions to ask include

a. Does it burn? Quickly or slowly?
b. If it burns, what sort of ash does it leave?
c. If it does not burn, what happens to it?
d. Does it shrivel or melt?
e. What sort of residue does it leave?
f. Is it unaffected by the flame?
g. If it burns or melts, is there a smell?

Classification is not too easy but children should, after a few experiments, be able to distinguish wool, and should be able to say whether or not a yarn is man-made — even if they cannot name it specifically — using Table 5.

5 Devise other ways of classifying yarns and fabrics.

Table 5

Type of fibre	Speed of burning	Appearance of residue	Smell
Wool, Silk	Burns slowly	Black, easily powdered ash	Unpleasant smell
Cotton, linen	Burns quickly	Grey, flaky ash	Little smell
Nylon, Acrilan	Shrivels and melts	End of burnt yarn is hard and smooth	Slight smell
Glass fibre	Melts	Hard bead formed	No smell

Spinning
6 Fibres twisted together are stronger than fibres on their own. Try twisting several fibres of hair together. Does this make a stronger thread than a single hair? How could this be tested? Try twisting fibres of sheep's wool, cotton wool or any other fibre available. Using a simple spindle (see Figure 21) try spinning some sheep's wool. (*Note*: Any fleece used by the children should be well washed. To make it easier for them to spin rub a little cooking oil into it.) To start spinning loop a piece of knitting wool as shown in the figure, hold the thread in one hand and twist the spindle with the other; as the fibres are pulled out the twist is transferred to them. Try and get someone to demonstrate spinning with a spinning wheel.

Structure of fabrics
7 Using string or very thick wool and large needles (made of lengths of dowel and sharpened at one end) knit several rows. If each row is knitted in a different colour, the looping of the yarn can be seen clearly. Look at the properties of knitted fabrics.

a. Do they stretch?
b. Do they keep their shape?
c. Are they firm or loose?
d. Are they warm? — **Keeping warm and keeping cool** (Section 12)
e. Can the yarns be looped together in different ways?

8 Using any sort of loom, from a board with nails hammered into it to a proper loom, make some simple woven fabric (under one thread and over another, like darning). Try ways of using warps with threads well-spaced or close together. Use different yarns for the weft. Try different patterns (e.g., under two threads and over one, or one row as darning and the next row over two and under two). Look at the properties of woven fabrics.

a. Do they stretch?
b. Do they keep in shape?
c. Can they be thick or thin?
d. What affects the pattern?
e. Is the fabric firm or loose?
f. What are the advantages of using woven fabrics?

Pull some fabrics to pieces and see how they are made. Yarns are very strong, and it is a waste of time asking children to try weaving with looms made of cardboard boxes or pieces of cardboard. It is always best to use wood.

Dyeing
9 Yarns or fabrics can be dyed using commercial dyes but it is more

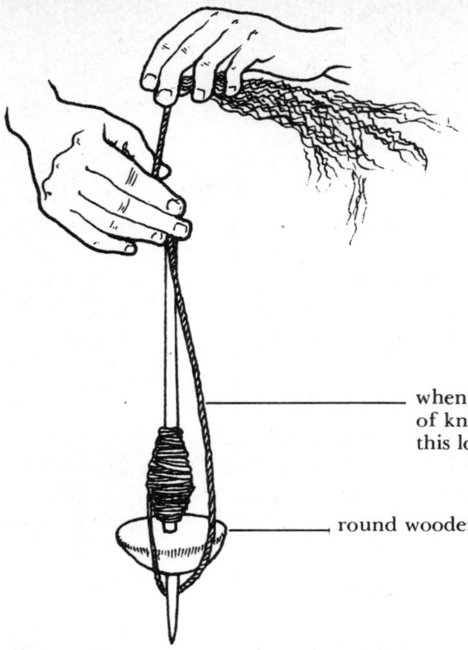

Figure 21 A hand-held spindle.

fun to try dyeing with natural products. The children will not be able to produce strong, bright colours but they can learn something about the history of dyeing, and there are many good books on this subject that can be used for reference.

10 Test for colour fastness by wetting the piece of fabric to be tested and then placing it between two pieces of white cloth (old sheeting is ideal) and pressing it with a hot iron. Does any of the colour come out on to the white cloth? Which colours are more likely to run?

Other properties of yarns

11 Other factors which children can investigate are shrinkage, water repellence, and wear. For all these they can think out their own experiments.

DEVELOPMENTS

1 Making collections of yarns and fabrics.
2 More work on dyes and dyeing — using mordants, natural dyes, chemical dyes.

3 Washing fabrics — a study of soaps and detergents.
4 Keeping silkworms.
5 Growing flax and cotton.

LINKS

1 History — the history of the wool and cotton industries, the story of man-made fibres.
2 Geography — the countries producing the different fibres (e.g., wool from Australia, cotton from USA, silk from China).
3 Craft — making a simple loom, tie dyeing, wax-resist dyeing (e.g., batik).
4 Art — looking at clothes and fabrics in pictures, embroidery all over the world, carpets from other countries (e.g., Turkey, Iran and China).

RESOURCES AND SUPPORT MATERIAL

Useful apparatus

Scissors, candles, long-handled tongs, wooden stands, G-clamps, small nets (type in which apples and nuts are bought), weights or washers, fleece, spindles (bought or home-made), small wooden boxes, pieces of wood (approximately 30 cm × 15 cm), pieces of old white cotton material, electric iron.

General reference books

A Handbook of Textiles A.M. Collier (Wheaton).
Plant Dyes (Ginn Practical Science Projects) I.F. Sime (Ginn).
Fibres and Fabrics J. Bird and E. Catherall (Macdonald Educational).

Children's books

Textiles J. Cochrane (ed.) (Macdonald Educational).
A First Look at Cloth R. Kerrod (Franklin Watts).
The Keeping of Animals and Plants in School V.B.A. Gregory (School Natural Science Society).
Yarn Crafts (Craft Series) (Macdonald Educational).

Other resources

1 Textile science pack — Nottingham Educational Supplies, 17 Ludlow Hill Road, West Bridgford, Notts NG2 6HD.
2 Small looms and spindles — Dryad Ltd, Northgates, Leicester LE1 4QR.
3 Cotton and flax seeds — Thompson and Morgan (address see Section 21).
4 Silk worms — World Wide Butterflies Ltd (address see Section 21).

17 Rocks and soils

Children always seem to be fascinated by rocks and fossils. Since stones, rocks and soils can be found in almost every environment they make interesting starters for a worthwhile scientific topic. Geological classification is extremely difficult, but a great deal can be learnt without expecting children to be able to name specimens or to get involved in technical details. They do, however, like the sound of words and so can be introduced to some names just for the fun of being able to say them! After all, such words as malachite, quartz, chalcedony and obsidian sound like something out of space fiction or a fantasy story.

GENERAL NOTES

1 A mineral is an inorganic substance found naturally and having definite physical characteristics. It can be identified by its particular properties and characteristics.

a. *Colour* — very definite in some minerals.
b. *Lustre* — the appearance of the surface. Some are glossy and others dull.
c. *Hardness* — hardness of minerals is measured on the Moh scale which ranges from one to ten. Something that can be scratched very easily with a pin has a hardness of one. A diamond has a hardness of ten.

2 A rock is a combination of two or more minerals. The Earth's crust is made up of rocks and minerals. Although children expect rocks to be hard, there are some soft ones; the one they are most likely to know is clay. This will harden as it dries and soften again when it gets wet.

3 Older children may like to know a little more about rocks generally and can appreciate a broad classification.

a. *Igneous rocks* — formed when molten rock cools and solidifies (e.g., basalt; granite).
b. *Sedimentary rocks* — formed when sediment is deposited from water (e.g., limestone, sandstone). This can be shown to them by shaking clay in water and then leaving it to settle.
c. *Metamorphic rocks* — those changed by heat and pressure (e.g., marble, slate).

4 An ore is a rock or mineral that contains enough of a metal to make it worthwhile extracting.
5 Some of the more easily identifiable rocks could be shown to children, named, and their properties discussed.

a. *Chalk* — sedimentary rock formed in shallow seas from the debris of marine creatures. It is evenly grained, soft and crumbles easily and is white. It contains microscopic fossils. No other rock looks like chalk.
b. *Sandstone* — sedimentary rock formed from grains of quartz. The grains are visible but bonded together. Its colour varies. It contains fossils and feels rough to the touch. In appearance, it is similar to grit. It is often used in buildings.
c. *Granite* — igneous rock formed below the Earth's surface. It is coarse-grained with visible crystals and is found in many colours (black and white, brown, pink, grey). It is a very hard rock and is used for building.
d. *Slate* — metamorphic rock formed from volcanic ash under intense pressure. It is smooth, fine grained, and is green, grey, blue or black in colour. Although very hard, it splits easily into thin pieces. No other rock is similar to slate. Its main use is for roofing slates because it can be split into thin, even slices.

6 Finely broken down rock mixed with organic material forms soil. Topsoil contains rocks and minerals, humus (decayed organic material), air, water and living organisms. It may vary in thickness from a few centimetres to many centimetres thick. Subsoil, unlike topsoil, contains no humus. The layers are shown in Figure 22. Again, this varies in thickness and lies above the bedrock. The composition of soils differs from area to area; a knowledge of this, drainage and climate is essential in agriculture.

ACTIVITIES AND EXPERIMENTS

Collections of rocks

1 Collections of rocks and stones can be made by the children. It does not matter whether or not the rocks are identifiable, but they can be classified according to colour, by general appearance or by the place where they were found. Each child in the class can be asked to bring in one piece of rock. Similar specimens can then be placed together.
2 Make a collection of rocks from a particular area. If this is kept small (a garden, a field or a small park) the collections can be put into boxes and comparisons made between areas.
3 Study a collection of named specimens of rock. How many of the names were familiar? Have the children ever seen similar rocks in a natural state?

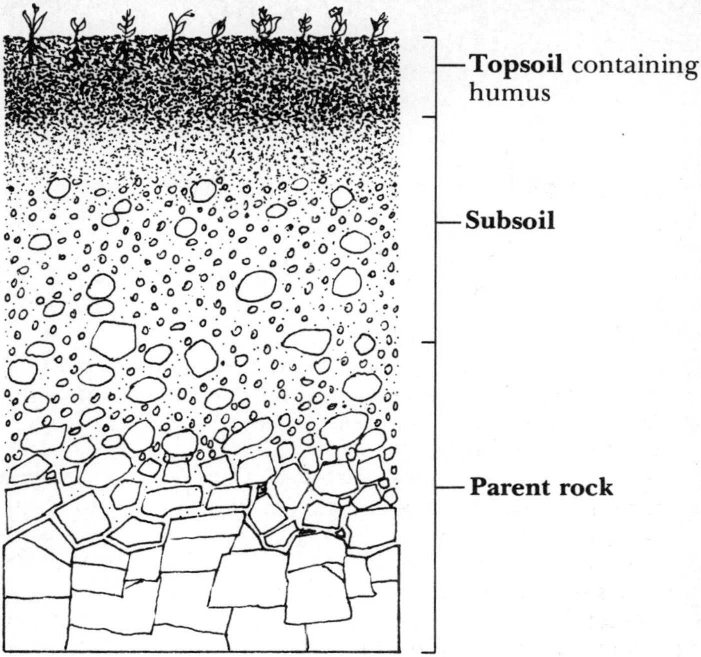

Figure 22 A soil profile.

4 Test rocks and stones for hardness using a pin, a nail, and a file.

a. Can the rock be scratched with a pin?
b. Can it be scratched with a nail?
c. Can a mark be made on it using a steel file?
d. Can it be broken with a hammer? – *Note*: If children are going to try this, they should wear protective goggles and the teacher should make sure that any children watching are well out of the way of flying pieces or are also wearing goggles.
e. Are any crystals obvious on the surface?
f. Can any be seen after breaking the rock?

5 Taking one known type of rock (e.g. slate or chalk) find out as much about it as possible.

Fossils
6 These can be seen at a local museum or can be collected by the children if they live in a suitable area. Some may be able to bring fossil specimens from home. Discuss how fossils were formed, and make artificial fossils using plaster of Paris. If a shell is pressed into plasticine, it leaves an impression which can be filled with plaster of

Paris. When the plasticine is removed a model of the shell, in plaster, is left. Here the plasticine is taking the place of the mud and silt into which the shells sank. Sometimes shells were filled with mud which hardened, and when the shell rotted away the cast of it was left.

Building materials

7 How many are natural rock and how many are made from artificial rock? (Cement, concrete, bricks, etc. count as artificial rocks. For example, although bricks are made from clay which is a natural rock, the clay has been treated in a way which alters its composition.)

8 Make a study of walls.

a. How many walls show signs of erosion?

b. Which are more susceptible to the growth of mosses and lichens?

c. How are the stones bonded together?

d. Are they made of natural or manufactured rock? If natural is it found locally?

9 Rocks can be looked at wherever the school is situated. Obviously, children living near a quarry or cliffs will have a better opportunity of looking at rock layers, but town children can study the rocks around them that are used as building materials. Is the church in the district fairly old? Is it built of sandstone blocks? Have any shops in the area got facing slabs made of polished marble? Are there any houses with slate tiles in the roof? Can you find any areas where pebbles are used for decoration? Where do you think these were found? They must have been rounded by the action of ice or water. Is broken rock being used for packing anywhere? Look at roads and railways. Look at the local churchyard — what are the tombstones made of? Are there any parts (such as steps) where constant wear has worn away the stones? How long has this taken? The children will have to find the date of the building for this.

10 Using clay find the effects of drying it, making it into bricks etc. What happens when the dried bricks get wet? Clay has to be fired if it is to be of use. If a kiln is not available, the children can make a very basic kiln in any place where they can dig a small hole and build a fire. Dig out a hole, a cube with each side about 40 cm long. Put a good layer of sawdust on the bottom and then pack in the clay objects to be fired. Firmly pack sawdust all round them so that they do not touch each other. Cover with a layer of sawdust about 6 cm deep and press down firmly. Now build a fire on the top of this and keep it going for about an hour. After that the sawdust should be smouldering and it should be left for 24 hours. At the end of this time, dig out the clay items, which should now be fired and therefore able to withstand water without disintegrating.

Soils
11 Samples from neighbouring areas can differ very considerably. If different soils are put in glass screw-top jars they can be compared. The amount of clay or sand in samples can be seen if a sample — three or four tablespoonfuls — is shaken up in a bottle of water. If it is then left to settle, the different constituents of the soils can be seen. Stones and gravel sink to the bottom, sand forms a layer on top of these and the last layer will be the fine particles of clay. The finest particles will probably remain suspended in the water for some time. Chalky soils will look white.

Gemstones
12 Gems are valuable minerals and are usually attractive. Examples include diamond, emerald, ruby, sapphire, aquamarine, garnet, amethyst, opal, turquoise and topaz. What colours are these stones? Where are they found?

DEVELOPMENTS

1 A closer look at rocks and rock forms.
2 Oil and petroleum.
3 Coal — formation, mining, uses.
4 The story of evolution — appearance of life on earth, and the first fossils.
5 Composition of soil, life in the soil, drainage.

LINKS

1 Geography — physical geography, formation of mountains.
2 History — prehistory, animals of the past.

RESOURCES AND SUPPORT MATERIAL

Useful apparatus
Storage boxes for rocks and stones, good hand lenses, clay, hammers, protective goggles, cement and sand, sawdust, glass jars with lids.

General reference books
Minerals and Rocks J. F. Kirkaldy (Blandford).
Rocks and Minerals H. S. Zim and P. R. Shaffer (Hamlyn).
Rocks T. Crisp (Nelson).
Junior Science Source Book J. W. Bainbridge *et al.* (Collins).
Fossils in Colour J. F. Kirkaldy (Blandford).

Children's books
Finding Fossils R. Hamilton and A. Insole (Kestrel Books).
Gold and Granite S. Brennand (Longman Young Books).

Other resources
1 Exhibits in museums — Geological Museum, Exhibition Road, London SW7; Natural History Museum, Cromwell Road, London SW7; City Museum, Congreve Street, Birmingham; National Museum of Wales, Cathays Park, Cardiff; University Museum, Parks Road, Oxford; Royal Scottish Museum, Chambers Street, Edinburgh. There are many museums with exhibits of rocks, fossils and gem stones, and many small local museums have excellent exhibits of the geology of their own area.
2 Rocks and minerals sets — Philip Harris Ltd (address see Section 21).
3 Fossil sets and fossil replicas — Philip Harris Ltd (address see Section 21).
4 Information about oil and the production of petroleum — Shell Education Service, Shell Centre, London SE1.
5 Films and other resources — BP Educational Service, PO Box 5, Weatherby, Yorkshire LS23 7EH.

18 Seashore and cliff

Not all children live near, or have the opportunity to visit, the seaside but they ought to be aware of the variety of living things associated with the shore line. Even a school trip lasting only a few hours can start off some interesting work, but obviously it is far better if the children can spend some time exploring this environment and discovering for themselves some of the plants and animals found there.

Regrettably much of the natural beauty of many beaches is being destroyed by the quantity of plastic rubbish that is constantly being washed ashore and — much more seriously — by the oil which is not only dirty and unsightly but is also responsible for the deaths of thousands of sea birds each year, and destroys many other animals and plants. Children should know about this and see the results for themselves because even if they can do little about the problem at the moment they may, in the future, be able to help with the conservation of some of the very varied coastal areas found round this country.

GENERAL NOTES

1 The shore is affected by the tides. (The cause of these can be another topic.) If children are going to visit the shore you will need to know the times of the high tides — not only from a safety point of view, but also so that you know when the maximum amount of beach is uncovered.

2 Rocky shores are probably the most interesting for children, because of the number of rock pools that can be found. All rock pools vary considerably in temperature and salinity. A small pool is soon warmed up by the sun and the water evaporates increasing the salt concentration (i.e. salinity). A heavy shower of rain will not only dilute the water but may also cool it.

3 It is almost possible to list all the plants and animals that may be seen; a good handbook will be almost indispensable (see the bibliography at the end of the section). A rock pool is a mini-environment and will give the children the chance to observe safely a great many marine plants and animals. They will probably find several of the following organisms.

a. Sea anemones — although plant-like, these are animals feeding on other water organisms. There are many different species.

b. Barnacles — both in the pools and on the rocks. There are hundreds of barnacles. They look quite dead when they are above the water line, but these strange crustaceans, once in the water, open and catch drifting food.
c. Shells (i.e. molluscs) — limpets (which remain almost stationary), periwinkles, topshells.
d. Crustaceans — crabs, shrimps, hermit crabs (living in various mollusc shells).
e. Tube worms — seen as white growths on stone, rocks and shells.
f. Fish — bullhead, blenny, young lumpsucker.
g. Starfish — not fishes at all but, like the sea urchin, they are echinoderms.

4 Although seaweeds are plants, they differ from land plants in many ways. They do not grow upright, but hang limply over rocks or float in the water. Many have to withstand being out of water for several hours and so have to have an effective method of conserving moisture. Also they need to remain fixed whatever the weather conditions. They have, therefore, adapted to the conditions in which they grow. Moisture is conserved by growing outside the tidal zone, growing in thick cushions so that the weeds underneath never get dry, growing in the shade of rocks and/or by lying flat on the rocks so that as small a surface as possible is exposed to the drying effects of sun and wind. Seaweeds are attached to rocks by a strong, root-like mass. This is not a root but a collection of shoots growing into the rough surface of the rock. Seaweeds that are likely to be found are various species of wrack, oarweeds, sea belts and sea bootlaces.

5 Sandy shores provide less protection; animals and plants, adapted for life among the rocks, will not thrive on a flat, sandy beach. Some animals can burrow into damp sand, so protecting themselves when the tide goes out. Examples are lugworms, and various bivalves (i.e. animals with a hinged, divided shell and a large 'foot' for digging such as razor shells, cockles, scallops).

6 Shingle beaches are very difficult habitats for living organisms. They are covered with pebbles of all sizes and those between the high and low-water marks are constantly moving. Silt and mud fill the crevices between the stones. Sandhoppers live underneath the pebbles; one species feeds on the rotting seaweeds left on the shore. Towards the top of the beach some plants (e.g., sea campion, sea couch) will be well established.

7 Sea birds are found all along the coast (e.g., oyster catchers, terns, gulls, ringed plovers, turnstones). These would make a special study on their own.

8 All along the beaches are found lines of stranded weeds and many other things left as the tide goes out. All manner of interesting items can be found here — driftwood, egg cases, bones, seaweeds, shells, dead sea birds, stranded crabs, jellyfish. Again, it is worth a special study.

9 The boundary of the shore may be marked by sand dunes or cliffs (there is always an area where the shore and the land meet and which has the characteristics of both). Many coasts are exposed and windy; here plant life is sparse.

a. Sand dunes are unlike any other coastal zones. A dune is an area of sand that is constantly being moved by the wind. It is only when the sand is held in place by plants such as sea couch and marram that it becomes a more or less permanent environment. Both these plants send out horizontal and vertical roots which bind the dunes together.

b. Plants that grow on rocky slopes and cliffs have to be able to cling to cracks and protuberances, and often have to withstand dry conditions. Some that can be looked for are sea plantain, sea kale, sea campion, glasswort, buckthorn, thrift, sea spurrey, sea lavender, samphire, sea purslane, gorse, sea holly and sandwort.

ACTIVITIES AND EXPERIMENTS

Selection of habitat

1 Studies of specific areas — a rock pool, sand dunes, the shore between the high-tide and the low-tide marks, a shingle beach, the strandline. Children could be divided into groups with each group looking at a different aspect of the same environment.

Collections

2 On a visit to the sea the children can decide for themselves what they want to study, but see that they are provided with plastic bags, boxes, bottles and buckets, small digging tools, hand lenses, fishing nets and a plastic tray for spreading out any specimens. Make sure that no glass containers are taken and that the children are taught the basic rules of collecting.

a. Replace any stones that are moved.
b. Never pull up plants. Take a small specimen only.
c. Replace live specimens in the place where they were caught.
d. Do not leave any litter.
e. Do not damage any gates, fences, bridges, walls, etc.

3 The children can collect shells in plastic bags or buckets but a few plastic boxes can be used for very small, fragile shells. Back at school, the shells should be soaked in a weak solution of household bleach for 24 hours, rinsed in clean water and left to dry. The shells can be stored in shallow cardboard boxes. If they are identified, the shell and the name label can be stuck into the box and the whole display covered with clingfilm.

4 Unless the school has a seawater aquarium, live specimens should be put into a bucket for a short time so that they can be looked at and then returned to the sea (or wherever found).

5 Interesting items — skate or dogfish egg cases (i.e. mermaid's purse), dried seaweeds, driftwood, pebbles, bones, fossils, crab shells, feathers — can be kept and labelled. Some driftwood may show signs of being attacked by the shipworm.

6 It is possible to press examples of some of the smaller seaweeds (do not try to preserve more than a small specimen). Wash the weeds in clean water, lay the sample on damp, thick drawing paper and leave to dry out for a few hours. Cover with a piece of waxed paper (the inner bag from a cornflakes packet will do very well), then several layers of newspaper. Put a board and something heavy on the top and leave for several weeks. Specimens can then be mounted as wanted. They look best if put onto thick card and are then covered with adhesive plastic film.

7 Although plant specimens can be collected and pressed, this is not really satisfactory. The plants take a long time to dry, and it means that the children tend to pick too many specimens. It is far better to collect just a few examples and draw them when back at school.

Animals

8 Look for animal tracks in the sand or bird footprints in silt and mud. Make casts of any clear, deep ones by pouring in plaster of Paris, (this can be taken to the beach in powder form, together with a small plastic bowl, an old spoon and a plastic bottle of water, and mixed on the spot.) The plaster is left to set until it can be lifted out. This will produce a cast of the track. To make the proper impression the cast can be taken back to school and, when well greased with petroleum jelly, have more plaster poured over it. When quite set this can be lifted off and you will have a proper impression of the track.

Make a seashore museum

9 Start with photographs of the site visited and add models, drawings and paintings made by the children. Show the specimens suitably mounted or displayed — a tray of sand makes a good base for shells and stones. Charts showing such things as the movement of periwinkles, bird counts (see Section 20) and profiles of rock pools will add to the interest. Label everything and add a taped commentary explaining the area and the work done. A slide projector with slides of seashore plants and animals can be put out for visitors to use.

10 Make rubbings (using thin, strong paper and a wax crayon) of flat shells, some seaweeds and leaves of cliff and dune plants.

Problem solving

11 Find the answers to the following questions.

a. If dry seaweed is put into water will it absorb water and swell up again?
b. How fast will a periwinkle or topshell move?
c. How many living animals can be found when digging out a marked area of sand?
d. How many different types of shells can be found in a given area?
e. On a shingle beach how many different animals and plants can be found?

DEVELOPMENTS

1 Life in the sea.
2 Other animals that live in shells.
3 A closer look at the rocks of the coast.
4 Setting up a marine aquarium.
5 Looking at estuaries.
6 Seasonal change.

LINKS

1 See also **Living in water** (Section 1), **Invertebrates and a snail study** (Section 6) and **Rocks and soils** (Section 17).
2 Geography — tides, times, phases of the moon, the seas of the world.
3 Mathematics — measurement of specimens, charts and counts of animals seen.
4 Physics — buoyancy and floating.

RESOURCES AND SUPPORT MATERIAL

Useful apparatus

Plastic bags and boxes, plastic buckets, fishing nets, hand lenses, spades, waxed paper, tape measures, binoculars, camera.

General reference books

The Seashore Naturalist's Handbook L. Jackman (Hamlyn).

The Sea Shore C. M. Yonge (Collins).
Pocket Guide to the Seashore J. Barrett and C. M. Yonge (Collins).
The Beach L. Jackman (Evans Brothers).
Coasts and Estuaries R. Barnes (Hodder and Stoughton).
Oxford Book of Invertebrates D. Nichols and J. Cooke (Oxford University Press).

Children's books

The Seashore E. Catherall (Wayland).
Seashore Animals G. Allen and J. Denslow (Oxford University Press).
Life on the Seashore D. Gilman (Macdonald Educational).
Sea and Estuary Birds J. Leigh-Pemberton (Ladybird Books).

Other resources

1 *The Edge of the Sea* (filmstrip) — VP Educational Resources, (address see Section 21).
2 *Exploring a Rocky Shore* (filmstrip) — Hugh Baddeley Productions (address see Section 21).
3 *Exploring a Sandy Shore* (filmstrip) — Hugh Baddeley Productions.

19 Exploring your environment

No school, wherever it is situated, is in such an environment that it is impossible to find suitable science topics. Although some schools have the obvious advantages of access to fields, forest, moorland, hills or the seashore, even the school built in the middle of an industrial city has its own particular world to be explored. It is, of course, almost impossible to separate environmental biology from environmental history and geography, and the suggestions made can include any, or all, of these.

Children like discovering things for themselves, but preparation is still needed. The teacher needs to know exactly what his or her area has to offer and needs to plan for the children's likely requirements. It must be appreciated that the environment can include the school building — both inside and outside — and that some of the work can be done when the weather is too bad for outdoor excursions. However, before you begin have a look round for yourself; look up as well as around! Roofs and chimneys are often overlooked, but they can teach a great deal about materials, shape and the history of buildings. Walk round the outside of the school grounds — even if these are only patches of asphalt surrounded by houses — and see how many living things you can find. Look for signs of wear and pollution, look at the walls or fences and think of questions that you could ask so that the children have to go and have a look before they can find the answer.

GENERAL NOTES

1 Ideas for indoor work include

a. Shapes, stresses and strains.
b. Windows, doors and other openings.
c. Materials — brick, concrete, glass, wood, plastic, metals, paint, paper.
d. Heating and lighting.

2 Ideas for work outside the school building include

a. Roofs and waterproofing, damp courses, pipes and drains.
b. Walls and brickwork.

c. Services going into the school — water, gas, electricity.
d. Playgrounds — plants and animals associated with the playground, trees, weeds (e.g., dandelion and willow-herb), mosses and lichens.

3 Outside the school the children could look at

a. Trees.
b. Streets, roads and lanes, other trackways.
c. Bridges, fences and walls, gates.
d. Ponds, pools, streams, canals.
e. Waste land, gardens, parks, hedges, fields.
f. Old buildings, churches and churchyards.

4 While there is a great deal to investigate, it is worth considering the possibilities of developing part of the area around school instead of just looking at what is already there. Schools with gardens or a field may benefit from the planting of some trees and before this is done suitable specimens will have to be found. The children can take an active part in the planting and can then watch the seasonal changes, and study the characteristics of their own trees.

The dreariest playground can be made more interesting; the building of a small, walled area can involve the children in shape, using materials such as cement and concrete, drainage, a study of soils and plant growth. Other ideas include

a. Making a weather station.
b. Building a pond (an old sink can be used if there are no other possibilities).
c. Making specialized gardens — herb garden, wild flower garden, butterfly and insect garden (by growing plants that will attract them), vegetable garden or a tree garden (by planting tree seeds or small saplings).

The books suggested at the end of this section provide a wealth of ideas and make very useful additions to any staff room library.

ACTIVITIES AND EXPERIMENTS

Looking at walls

1 *Bricks* — look at the brick pattern and find the commonest brick bonds in the area. Try wall building using bricks and concrete. It would be more interesting to try wall building for some purpose, but it is worth children finding out that some ways of putting bricks together will not stand up to ordinary wear and tear.

2 *Damp courses* — why does water not constantly creep up the walls of buildings? Look at the damp course of a building. What is it? Place a house brick in a bowl of water so that the water comes half way up one side. Place a dry brick on top and see what happens. How can the water be prevented from creeping from one brick to another? If an impermeable layer (e.g., plastic sheeting) is placed in between, the water cannot pass through.

3 *Stone walls* — what type of stone was used? What is a dry stone wall? How is it built? How is stone cut so that it can be used for building? What stones were used for building castle walls?

4 *Wall features* — look for wall straighteners, sundials and date stones. Date stones will enable children to find out the age of the wall. They can then compare such things as plant growth and erosion on walls built at different times.

5 Look at the living organisms associated with a particular wall. How many plants can be found? Make a chart showing what can be found; the following example lists a few of the things that could be looked for on an old brick churchyard wall.

	Dandelion	**Moss**	**Ivy**	**Grass**
Growing at the base	√		√	√
Growing at the top	√			√
Growing from cracks				√
Climbing			√	
Growing on the surface of the stone		√		

How many small animals can be found on the surface or in cracks? How many can be found at the base?

Walks, paths and trackways

6 Look at the natural history of any path that can be visited (and included in this will be roads and streets) and ask the following questions.

a. How old is it?

b. Is it a deliberately made trackway or has it appeared because of constant usage?

c. Are there any trees? Are they growing naturally or have they been cut or lopped?

d. Are there any signs of pollution? Make plant charts of the trackway. Are there many different types of plants? Were they planted or did they get there naturally? Are there any signs of animal life? What are these? Make a plan of the trackway marking in all the plants found.

A study of shapes

7 Look at shapes seen along a street or road. Look for particular shapes and decide whether or not the shape is important or merely decorative. Examples include

a. Round manhole covers.
b. Five-barred gates — those with five horizontal bars and a diagonal running from one corner to another.
c. Arch bridge.
d. Triangular shape of a roof gable.
e. Cylindrical shape of a pillar box.

Plant habitats

8 Look at roofs, gutters, railway bridges, cracks in the pavement or the playground, fences or barns. Find plants that are growing in unusual places. How did the seeds get there, and how do the plants survive without soil? What plants will grow in such unlikely habitats?

9 Make a study of one plant that is found near the school — the dandelion grows almost anywhere and is easily recognizable. Is the dandelion plant growing on its own or in a group? How did the seeds get there? How far will a dandelion 'parachute' fly from the parent plant? How long does it take the seed to germinate? Are there any places where, apparently, it will not grow?

10 Some children may have observed the colonization of waste land and noticed that gradually plants begin to grow and cover the ground. Dig out a patch of garden or field, fencing it round with sticks and string. Remove all signs of plant life and leave it. How soon is it before plants begin to grow? How did they get there? What are they? This can be done equally well using an old sink or plastic bowl. Does this colonization take place in towns as well as in more open areas? How long does it take before the surface of the soil is more or less covered with growing plants? Does the weather or season affect the speed of colonization?

Animal habitats

11 Look at the habitats of small animals — spiders, earwigs, woodlice, labybirds, slugs — and try and find out what they feed on. Spiders appear to live in the most unlikely places but they must find their food somewhere. (Children usually assume that all spiders are web spinners so this could be used as a starter for some further work on spiders.)

12 Collect some of the small animals and look at them with a good hand lens or a binocular microscope. Make a trap by putting bits of fruit in the bottom of a plastic pot. Bury this up to the top and cover with a flat stone, resting on a small pebble to allow a space to admit any small animals out food hunting.

Edges and verges
13 Country roads offer more scope for investigation than town streets, but both can pose some problems for the children to solve. What effect does cutting have on grass verges? Does it destroy any natural habitats? Does traffic pollution affect plant growth? How well are any trees growing? Has anything affected their growth? — lopping, damage from vehicles that have hit them or rubbed them, nails driven into them for various reasons, growing against or near a wall or fence). What are the commonest plants?

Other ideas
14 Several other activities may be pursued by the children.

a. Study of a patch of lawn.
b. Wind and weather.
c. Animal visitors — including domestic animals.
d. Water — streams, ponds, muddy areas, places where puddles collect.

DEVELOPMENTS

1 Looking at the immediate environment, it is almost impossible to avoid the history of the area and it would be a waste to do so. If the children are looking at an old wall or hedge, it becomes much more interesting if they find out how old it is and who put it there.
2 Seasonal changes in the area.
3 A closer look at domestic animals.
4 Furniture and the materials from which it is made.
5 Pollution and conservation.

LINKS

1 History — the history of the area or the building being studied.
2 Geography — maps and plans of the area, importance of a nearby river or canal.
3 Mathematics — bird and animal counts, shape, tesselation and symmetry.
4 Social studies — talk to old people who have lived near the school for a long time (they often know a surprising amount about the area and their personal stories are well worth recording).

RESOURCES AND SUPPORT MATERIAL

Useful apparatus

Tape measures and rules, bags and boxes for collections, large plastic bowls, buckets, gardening tools, wax crayons, string, camera, tape recorder.

General reference books

Bellamy's Backyard Safari D. Bellamy and T. Bellamy (BBC Publications).
Urban Ecology D. Gilman (Macdonald Educational).
Natural History of the Garden M. Chinery (Collins).
Using the Environment:Investigations 1 and 2; Tackling Problems 1 and 2; Ways and Means Science 5/13 (Macdonald Educational).
Wild Life in Towns G. Carter (Macdonald Educational).

Childen's books

Nature in the Town H. Stanton (Ladybird Books).
Nature in Towns (New Reference Library) (Macdonald Educational).
Conservation J. Whinray (A. & C. Black).
Street Flowers R. Mabey (Kestrel Books).
Town Animals F Hall (Puffin Books).

Other resources

1 *Local Studies Kit* by Philip Sauvain — Macmillan Education (address see Section 21).
2 *Mini-Environment*: *Walls, Churchyards, Footpaths* (filmstrips) — The Slide Centre (address see Section 21).
3 *Life Around Farms and Fields* (filmstrip) — The Slide Centre.
4 *Hedgerow Wildlife, Motorway Wildlife, Urban Wildlife* (wallcharts) — Studio Two Educational (address see Section 21).

20 Counting, sampling and solving

Not all the science that young children can do necessarily involves comprehensive topics. Some very small-scale pieces of work can be equally valuable, and it helps if children are used to counting, measuring, sampling and working out ways of solving problems. Also, if time is short, a brief investigation can be done with reasonable ease. This could, if handled properly, teach the children how to carry out minor pieces of research and to record the results in a clear and sensible way. It also shows them how to record their results in such a way that they can be easily understood by other children — see **Mathematics and nature**. (Section 3)

SIMPLE COUNTS

1 The children can make a bird count.

a. Count the birds seen in a particular area (such as the school playground) over a timed period. This can be compared with either a count of the same duration made in another area or with a count done in the same place, but at a different time of the day or under different weather conditions.

b. Make a count of the types of birds seen in a specific area over a fixed period of time. This necessitates the children being able to identify the birds likely to be seen. The following table provides an example.

Birds seen on the school field on May 2nd: 10:00–12:00						
Sparrow	Starling	Magpie	Blackbird	Rook	Others	Total seen

If such a count is carried out on several days, the children can decide which are the commonest birds of the area.

2 With the gradual loss of suitable habitats such animals as the frog and newt are becoming increasingly rare in many areas. It would be interesting to find places where they are managing to survive, or even managing to increase. Make a frog count of the immediate environment and involve children from other schools in other districts. Compare results and plan ways in which these animals could be protected in those areas where they seem to be dying out. Even very small-scale conservation projects (such as building a school pond) are worth considering. Obviously the species of endangered animals will vary from place to place and the children can find out if there are any projects locally, or nationally, to protect them.

Averages

3 This is particularly useful as it applies mathematical concepts to biological topics.

a. Count the number of petals on daisies. Are there always the same number? Count the number on ten flowers. Find the average number of petals. How many times do the children consider they will have to do this to get a reasonably accurate average?

b. Measure the hand span of all the children in the class. Work out the average span. Is it possible to draw any conclusions from this? Do tall children have a hand span above average?

SAMPLING

Collecting information

1 If children are setting out to collect information, they must be quite clear as to what is actually wanted and what they have to do. If the work involves collecting specimens, they must understand what they can take and what they must leave alone.

Making profiles

2 Decide on the stretch of ground where the profile is to be made and decide on the length of the line. Put in a stake at each end and stretch a strong string between the two, making sure that it is perfectly level by using a spirit level (see Figure 23). Using a metre ruler measure the distance between the ground level and the string; do this every 20–30 cm so that a plan can be drawn on squared paper. Sketch in the plants in the right positions (symbols can be used). Compare profiles made in several places.

3 Look at walls and fences and collect information about algae and lichens. (The children do not need to identify these by names.) Do these grow only on stone surfaces? Why are some surfaces more prone to growth than others? Does the surface have to be old before these plants begin to grow? Do they damage the surface? Look at

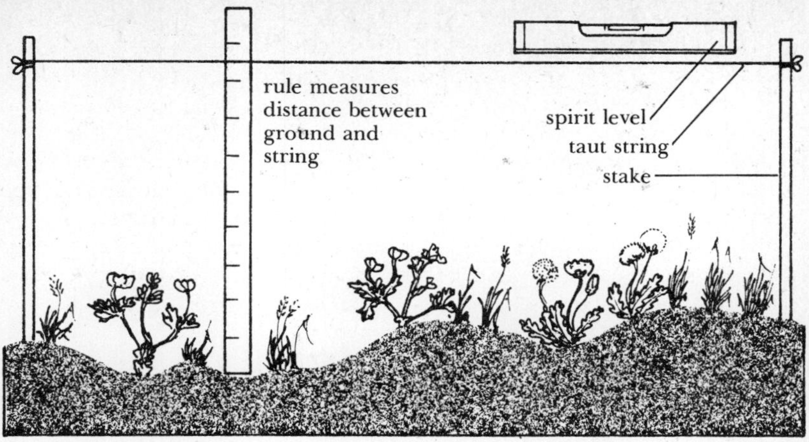

Chart of ground profile

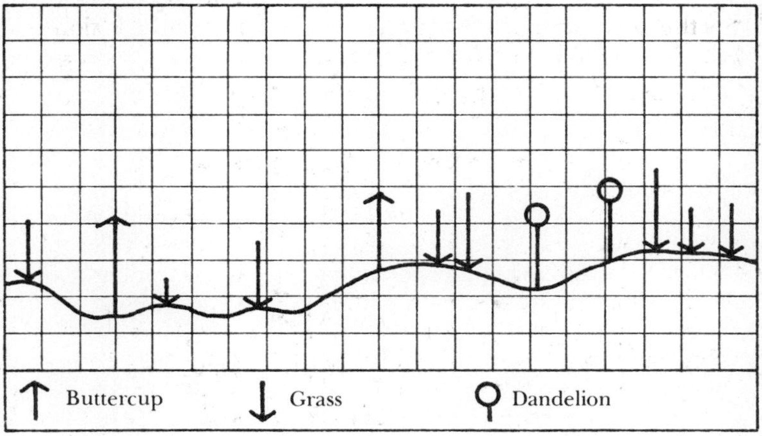

Figure 23 Making a ground profile.

trees and find out if algae grows equally well all over the trunk. What affects the growth?

4 List all the animals seen near the school during one week. The children can take it in turns to act as the observer. Include domestic pets as well as any wild mammals, birds, amphibians or insects. Try to decide why the animals are in the area. Is the presence of animals associated with feeding? Work out some of the possible food chains and see if there is any connection between the visitors and possible feeding habits. For example

Nettles → caterpillars → sparrow → sparrow hawk
Rose bushes → greenfly → ladybirds → insect-eating birds

Examples of sampling

1 Mark out a definite area of ground (say a 50 × 50 cm square) and put strings every 10 cm from left to right and from top to bottom so that 25 smaller squares are formed. Make an accurate count of all the plants seen, marking them on a chart (the guide strings will help). The children can also call out their finds to a partner using coordinates.

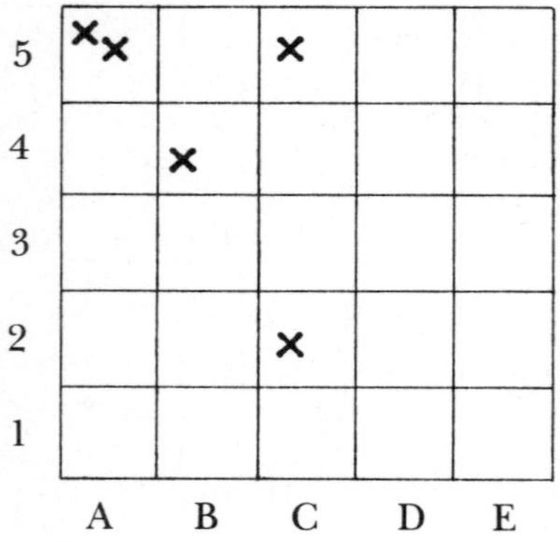

each cross represents a clover — found in squares A5, B4, C2 and C5

If several groups of children do this they can pool the results and can make a list, in rank order, of the plants found. What was the commonest plant? Was this plant found all over the area or only in, say, shaded parts?

2 Find the commonest hair or eye colour of all the children in your school. To do this the children need to take a random sample. They could do this by registering the colour of every tenth child as the school goes in to assembly or they could use the numbers on the class register. If there are 30 children in the class, put cards numbered 1—30 in a box. Pick out one card for every five or ten children (or fraction of five or ten). Look for this number in the register and record the colouring of the child indicated. If a quarter of this sample are found to have light brown hair is it true to say that 25 percent of children in the school have light brown hair? The children can discuss this and can see if there are better ways of carrying out such an investigation.

SETTING PROBLEMS

These give children the opportunities to work out ways of solving problems, and to work in ways of their own choosing. The problems can either be suggested by the children while doing other work — after an outing or after seeing a film or reading something in a book — or they can be set by the teacher, but they need to have a definite outcome and be worth doing.

Examples

1 Devise some way of finding out what sort of food will best attract wild birds to a bird table or garden.

2 Decide on some small animal that the children are likely to find (e.g., snail, earwig, woodlouse, centipede, periwinkle, spider) and find what sort of habitat it likes best.

3 If woodlice are moved a short distance from the stone under which they were found, will they go back to that place? Do they tend to stay in the same place? Woodlice can be marked with a tiny dab of nail varnish so that their movements can be traced as far as possible.

4 What affect does the tide have on small shore environments (e.g., a small rock pool, a single rock, a small stretch of sandy beach or shingle). Does the movement of the sea alter the population of the area?

5 What effect does the acidity of the soil have on the growth of plants? Do some plants prefer acid soil? Use pH indicator papers to test acidity. (The pH is a measure of the degree of acidity.) Soil-testing kits can be bought from garden centres and shops selling gardening supplies. Increasing pH values indicate more alkaline conditions.

pH value	**3–4**	**5–6**	**7**	**7–8+**
meaning	very acid	slightly acid	neutral	alkaline

6 Problems need not be biological but they should always necessitate the children experimenting or making direct observations.

a. How well are biscuits packaged? Do the packages keep the biscuits fresh? Do they prevent the biscuits being damaged? Will the packaging withstand damp or heat?

b. Which type of floor coverings best stand up to heavy wear and tear? Devise ways of testing coverings.

c. A ball will bounce but is it possible to bounce an egg without breaking the shell? To do this the children will first have to find out something about bouncing and the properties of materials.

GENERAL REFERENCE BOOKS

School Projects in Natural History Devon Trust for Nature Conservation (Heinemann).
Tackling Problems, Using the Environment Science 5/13 (Macdonald Educational).
Rainbow Fact Book of Science M. Dempsy (ed.) (Grisewood and Dempsy).
Metals, 1 and 2 Science 5/13 (Macdonald Educational).
The Seaside Naturalist's Handbook L. Jackman (Hamlyn).
Like and Unalike, 1, 2 and 3 Science 5/13 (Macdonald Educational).

21 Books and other resources

REFERENCE BOOKS

Most of these have already been mentioned in the text but they are particularly useful sources of information.

Bainbridge, J. W. *et al. Junior Science Source Book* (Collins).
Bisacre, M. (ed.) *Science and Technology* (Marshall Cavendish).
Bishop, O. *Adventures with Small Animals* (John Murray).
Chinery, M. *Field Guide to the Insects of Britain and Northern Europe* (Collins).
Dempsy, M. (ed.) *Rainbow Fact Book of Science* (Grisewood and Dempsy).
Department of Education and Science *Keeping Animals in Schools* (Her Majesty's Stationery Office).
Devon Trust for Nature Conservation, *School Projects in Natural History* (Heinemann Educational Books).
Finch, I. *Science Workshop Books, 1 and 2* (BBC/Longman).
Gilbert, C. and Matthews, P. *Look! Primary Science* (Addison-Wesley).
Imrie, J. *Using the Microscope* (A. & C. Black).
Jackman, L. *The Seaside Naturalist's Handbook* (Hamlyn).
Mackean, D. G. *Introduction to Biology* (John Murray).
Mitchell, A. *Trees of Britain and Northern Europe* (Collins).
Mourier, H. and Winding, O. *Wild Life in House and Home* (Collins).
Sauvain, P. *Looking Around in Town and Country* (Watts).
Saville, M. *Exploring a Wood* (Transworld Publications).
Science 5/13 *Using the Environment:Investigations 1 and 2*; *Tackling Problems 1 and 2* ; *Ways and Means* (Macdonald Educational).
Science 5/13 *Metals, 1 and 2* (Macdonald Educational).
Showell, R. *Looking at Insects and Small Animals* (Ladybird Books).
Showell, R. *Teaching Science to Infants* (Ward Lock Educational).
UNESCO *Source Book for Science Teaching* (UNESCO Educational Publications).
Windridge, C. *General Science Books, 1—5* (Schofield and Sims).

USEFUL ADDRESSES

Slides and filmstrips
The Slide Centre, 143 Chatham Road, London SW11 6SR.
Hugh Baddeley Productions, Education Distribution Centre, 8 Brampton Road, St. Albans, Herts.
VP Educational Resources, The Green, Northleach, Cheltenham GL54 3EX.
Diana Wylie, 3 Park Road, London NW1 6XP.

Films (free loan)
British Gas Film Library, Park Hall Road Trading Estate, London SE21 8EL.
Unilever Educational Productions, PO Box 68, Unilever House, London EC49 4BQ.

Wallcharts
Macmillan Educational, Houndmills, Basingstoke, Hampshire RG21 2XS.
Nature Conservancy Council, Attingham Park, Shrewsbury, Shropshire SY4 4TW.
Studio Two Educational, 6 High Street, Barkway, Royston, Herts.
Frederick Warne Ltd, 40 Bedford Square, London WC1B 3HE.

General suppliers of science apparatus and materials
ESA Ltd, School Materials Division, Pinnacles, PO Box 22, Harlow, Essex.
Philip Harris Ltd, Lynn Lane, Shenstone, Staffordshire WS14 0EE.
Osmiroid Educational (for measuring equipment and lenses), Osmiroid Works, Gosport, Hampshire.

Living material
Thompson and Morgan, Ipswich, Suffolk IP2 0BA.
World Wide Butterflies Ltd, Over Compton, Sherborne, Dorset.

Other addresses
Countryside Commission, 1 Cambridge Gate, Regents Park, London NW1 4JY.
Forestry Commission, Information Branch (Schools), 231 Corstorphine Road, Edinburgh H12 7AT.
Natural History Museum, Cromwell Road, London SW7.
Royal Society for Nature Conservation, The Green, Nettleham, Lincoln LN2 2NR.
Royal Society for the Protection of Birds, Education Department, The Lodge, Sandy, Bedfordshire SG19 2DL
School Natural Science Society Publications, 44 Claremont Gardens, Upminster, Essex RM14 1DN.

Index